Collecting British Toby Jugs

Vic Schuler

Edited by Francis Salmon

Third Edition

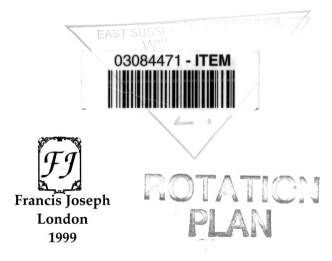

FJ

Francis Joseph
London
1999

Acknowledgments

The following are warmly thanked for their help in producing this book:
Mr Bailey of Blakeney Art Pottery; Malcolm Bannister; Paul Barthaud (Christies of South Kensington); Winston Bartold; Stella Beddowes (Brighton Museum and Art Gallery); Judi Bland (Hayford Antiques); Wilf Blandford; Mark Bolton; Margaret Broderick; E. Myra Brown (Liverpool Museum); John Burgess; Elizabeth Caper (Tony Wood (Studio 82) Ltd.); Frederick Chavez; Chris Cole; Peggy Davies; Audrey Dudson; Judy & Malcolm Dyer; R. Feldman Ltd. (London Silver Vaults); Anton Gabszewicz (Christies of King Street); Justin Garrard (Phillips of London); Diana and Ray Ginns; Geoffrey A. Godden; John Gould (Gladstone Museum, Longton); Joy Hallam; W. W. Hamilton; Mick Haskel, Foyn; Stephen Helliwell (Christies of South Kensington); Jonathan Horne; Pat Halfpenny (City Museum and Art Gallery, Stoke on Trent); Neil Inwood; Terry Ledwith; Jocelyn Lukins; Lady Gwynneth Mackintosh; Elizabeth Julie McWilliams; Frank Mayer; Pauline and John Meredith; Arnold Mountford (City Museum and Art Gallery, Stoke on Trent); Stephen Mullins (Chicago Jug Museum); The Nelson-Atkins Museum of Art, Kansas City; Peter Parr; H. Peroyetz Ltd. (London Silver Vaults); Phillips of Bath; Robin Price; Elaine and John Robinson; Francis Salmon; Jennifer Shaw; Dora Shaw (Wood and Sons Burslem); C.B. Sheppard & Sons; Dr Paul Sing (Staffordshire Fine Ceramics); Derek Smith; Peter Smith; Ron Smith; Rita Smythe (Britannia); Sotheby's of London; Les Steer; Tracy Still; Walter Tatlock; Brian Toby; Doug Tootle; Dr Sydney Wain; Peter Williams (Sotheby's of Chester); Wintertons of Litchfield; Vera and Sidney Wright.

ISBN 1-870703-28-6

Published by Francis Joseph,
5 Southbrook Mews, London SE12 8LG
Tel: 0181 318 9580

Photographs: Trevor Leak

Scanning: Gabriel Granger

Typesetting by
E J Folkard Computer Services
199 Station Road, Crayford, Kent DA1 3QF

Printed by Greenwich Press Ltd
Eastmoor Street, London SE7 8LX

Front cover photograph: Shield Toby

To my wife Peggy who
recently passed away

Preface

The classic Toby Jug figures wore eighteenth-century style clothes, so to the purist, any deviation might seem to be erroneous. We have moved on 200 years, and dress styles have changed; so with the passing of time I feel that any jug in the form of the complete figure of man or woman should still be called a Toby Jug, even with the modern mode of dress.

Prices where possible have been indicated in this volume. Collectors must be aware that prices are general, and do not take into account the margins that dealers and antique shops need to apply in order to provide collectors with a service. Auctioneers in the UK, take a percentage or a commission, which is VATable, and at auction you do not know if you will receive the full realisable price. In short, the prices given are the possible sale price, but they are not the prices that you, the collector should expect to sell your piece for.

In any case, it is the market itself that determines prices. If you as a collector want a piece, it is down to your own ingenuity to get hold of it at the lowest possible price and, if you want a £20,000/$30,000 Astbury Fiddler Midshipmite you might well have to get your wallet out — or maybe go for a Ralph Wood or a modern Kevin Francis piece instead.

It is too difficult to price an 'ordinary' Toby owing to the great variation of quality, condition, age and desirability, and we don't know what the future will bring in collecting fashions, although over the past 200 years Toby Jugs seem to have steadily risen in value. Due to the lack of Tobies coming up for auction, it is almost impossible to put a value on many jugs.

Jugs in the form of animals such as cats, dogs, bears and monkeys have not been included.

Since the publication of the second edition of *British Toby Jugs* in 1994, old Tobies have appeared and new ones have been produced most notably by Kevin Francis.

There has been one recent major Toby Jug auction sale, held by Christies of King Street, St James, London. This was the collection formed by the Fourth Marquess of Bute. Before 1920, the formation of this collection was contemporary with that of Capt R. K. Price, who formed his collection between 1907-1917. They must have known each other. This has provided invaluable reference.

The other important Toby sale, this century was that of Lord Mackintosh of Halifax, the head of the toffee firm, who died in 1964. It was reported in the press at the time of his death, that he had collected Toby Jugs for 25 years, but, I know that he used to visit Capt Price at his house in the 1920s. Capt Price died in 1929. If the newspaper report was correct, it looks as if Lord Mackintosh stopped collecting long before his death.

The Mackintosh auction held by Sotheby's in May and October 1967, was the most important Toby Jug sale up to that date, 93 jugs. But the Bute auction outshines the Mackintosh sale in number 208 jugs, but the condition of many, if not most, left a lot to be desired. The Mackintosh collection appeared to be undamaged. Nevertheless in the main, good prices were maintained. I have always said that a true collector will always accept some damage to pottery that is around 200 years old. But it was noticeable that the Midshipmite and Fiddler Tobies had dropped in price dramatically since 1988. Other early tobies like the Ralph Wood's though, have maintained their value in general and many have increased by an average of about 20%.

Twentieth century toby jugs in particular are fetching very good sums of money and the Kevin Francis interest has been phenomenal. It is fair to say that Kevin Francis tobies are the Ralph Wood's of the twentieth century.

Contents

About the Author

Victor Hugo Schuler was born in 1918 at Badshot Lea, Surrey, and spent most of his early childhood in Surrey and Sussex with his grandparents; his grandfather being a downland shepherd. He moved to his parents' home in London in 1926, and married in 1946.

For fifty years Vic was a tool and die maker, retiring in 1982, but his main interest throughout his life has been British history and antiques. His major obsession, not surprisingly, has been Toby Jugs which he has collected for the past 40 years.

In the early thirties he took up an avid interest in blues and jazz, collecting many records and pursuing this interest to the ultimate, moving to America from 1948 to 1950 and meeting many of the great pioneer jazz musicians.

On returning to England his new obsession became English windmills, and he travelled the country in search of these for many years with his wife Peggy.

For thirty-five years Vic had a Saturday stall at the Portobello Road Market in London, unmistakable in his 'Toby' tricorn hat, selling general antiques, bric-a-brac, and, of course, Tobies.

Vic Schuler is a confessed romantic who likes nothing modern and thinks we are living in an age of ugly buildings, slovenly clothes and tuneless music. In spite of growing up through the depression of the Twenties and Thirties, he would not have missed a moment of it!

Foreword

A short history of Kevin Francis by Francis Salmon

Vic and I have become enormous friends over the past 15 years – since the very first edition of *Collecting British Toby Jugs*. It was this book which inspired my erstwhile partner, Kevin Pearson, and myself, to go into toby jug production. Whilst I no longer have any interest in the Kevin Francis business, I am delighted by the recent success of the range we introduced, and, of course those still in production today at the thriving pottery of Peggy Davies Ceramics.

Initially Kevin and myself were unlikely partners. I was lecturing in Economics, Kevin was in advertising. We had been college friends though, and when I saw Kevin's first book on character jugs, published by Cresswell, I was impressed and I set about forming a publishing company to do Kevin's other books. I asked Kevin to join me as partner and we merged our names to form Kevin Francis (Francis Kevin didn't sound so good!). This was in 1983, when we were both around 25 years of age – quite young to be developing the business we did.

It wasn't long before Kevin got restless, and he commissioned the first toby, of Vic himself – produced by the talented Peggy Davies. Peggy, the well known and highly esteemed modeller for Royal Doulton, was spending her last few years working freelance, and she was delighted to take on the work. The result was quite breathtaking. I knew instinctively that we were onto a winner. The edition sold out in no time and the scene was set for a whole range of toby jugs. Kevin commissioned the Doctor, Cook, Postman, Gardener and the Shareholder from a delighted Rod Davies, thus formally making our relationship with Peggy and Rod a business that was built on a solid basis. I felt we needed more subjects of character, and I soon commissioned Peggy to make a Winston Churchill with a lion at his side. This sparked a series of Churchills, but I still think Peggy's is the best. With failing health, Peggy was unable to cope with the demands for more models, and turned to the services of Douglas V Tootle and Andy Moss for future models. Kevin's Gorbachev was a real coup, as the Berlin Wall was coming down, and I was able to make the trip to Berlin for some genuine pieces of wall for that toby jug. I came up with the idea for the Clarice Cliff toby and the subsequent Artists and Potters Series after discussing Art Deco character jugs with my old friend Howard Watson. The result was quite spectacular, with the Clarice Cliff selling out from a simple line drawing in one of my newsletters. In fact, Howard's drawings of character jugs were eventually used for an art deco series and I thought the results were superb. Doug Tootle had done a very innovative job in his design of the Clarice Cliff, and thus he secured a number of new commissions. Moving to his own premises in Liverpool Road, Rod Davies was fast proving to be among the best quality potters in Stoke.

After this though, good ideas became difficult to come by. We had some excellent models from Geoff Blower with his King Henry VIII and the Shakespeare, but the subject matter just wasn't as strong as the earlier series. Andy Moss also came up with some excellent designs for my Artists series, and I think the Salvador Dali is still my favourite, but the with the recession of the early 1990s and the need to keep up production come what may, the company started to struggle. We decided that a three way split was the most appropriate way forward. I kept the publishing business. It had been my first love and I felt I could keep it going until the recession was over. This I did and hence books like these under the new company name – Francis Joseph. Kevin always leaned to the ceramics side of the business, but something had to give, he was living and working in America, and was soon to marry, so he kept the American side of the business – something he had plugged at from the very beginning of the partnership. Finally, Rod was to keep the Kevin Francis UK ceramics business. All of us have gone on to a fair degree of success, so the arrangements set in motion have worked out extremely well for all concerned. I wish all the very best of luck to the people that have made the Kevin Francis range a success, especially Kevin and Rod who worked so hard to make it happen. And I must mention Mike Pepper who has so often come up with imaginative designs for Kevin Francis, particularly the colour trials of each piece, Dave the glazing and firing man, Andy the handy man, Mike the fettler, Reece Davies the super salesman, and Heather who keeps them all under control – well, she tries.

Just think. If it were not for Vic, there would be no Kevin Francis pottery and probably no book on toby jugs to date!

See the next page for just one example of the kind of coverage we got in the early 1990s.

Election proves a jug's game

by Louise Hidalgo

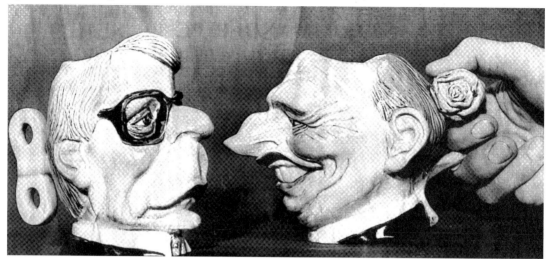

The election campaign was enlivened yesterday with the release of jugs bearing the less than flattering images of Messrs Kinnock and Major made famous by the *Spitting Image* television comedy.

Initial orders show Mr Major outselling his opponent by four to three. Kenneth Clarke, the education secretary, was among the first of a number of former MPs to place a £100 order for the pair.

The tradition of such images dates back to the 18th century, although the more famous Toby jugs – full length portraits – began even earlier. The Duke of Wellington earned himself a "character" mug after the battle of Waterloo.

Sir Winston Churchill crossed swords with Royal Doulton over its mug of him produced during the second world war, and ordered production to cease. One of the 300 mugs that slipped on to the market fetched £15,000 at auction last year.

Similarly, a modern day war hero, General Norman Schwarxkopf, was angered by the commemorative image produced by Kevin Francis of Stoke-on-Trent, makers of the Kinnock-Major pair. The firm has agreed to stop sales to the US.

Article which appeared in The Times, *Friday 20 March 1992 and reproduced with kind thanks.*

CHAPTER ONE

Collecting Toby Jugs

There are still lots of Toby Jugs about but the ones found in 'junk' shops tend to be just that. Apart from the occasional lucky break, you only get what you pay for, and the lucky breaks are few and far between. However hope springs eternal and we collectors cannot be deterred from spending our time in junk shops and markets, in spite of the odds against us. There will always be a possibility of the great 'find' which justifies such disproportionate efforts.

The following is an extract from R.P. Way's Antique Dealer* about his efforts to obtain a very nice Toby Jug just before the First World War. He had just sent some 'Ralph Wood' figures to Captain Price, whom he knew to be an avid collector of Toby Jugs:

'. . . A friend of mine in Bath asked me whether I would know a Ralph Wood Toby Jug if I saw one. I said I hoped so and he asked me to go with him to Swanage in Dorset. He told me to dress up as smartly as I could, because he had an idea that he would explain to me later. I was extremely puzzled, but I met him the following Saturday at the station wearing my best clothes, yellow wash-leather gloves and a swinging Malacca cane with a silver top.

In the train he explained that the jug belonged to a sullen, bad-tempered innkeeper. The inn was a small one in an out-of-the-way part of Swanage. He knew the man didn't want to part with the jug, but he thought that if I came on the scene, as a rich looking type with money, and if the jug was a good one, I might impress the innkeeper into making a deal.

We got to the inn between five and six o'clock and ordered drinks. My friend took the landlord aside and explained to him what an important customer I was and then he asked him to have a drink with us.

The drinks turned out to be several rounds and then the landlord was asked if he would mind showing me his old jug. Mellowed by what he had taken the landlord said, 'Certainly, but 'e ain't for sale mind, 'es willed away 'e is.'

When I saw the jug I knew at once that it was a very fine example of Ralph Wood's work, brilliant, absolutely perfect and it even had its original cover, on which R.K. Price was so keen. The face was aubergine, the coat a rich blue and breeches deep yellow. It was a beauty.

While I examined it the landlord rambled on '. . . an' would you believe it, guv'nor, I bin offered £10 for that old jug, daft, ain't it?'

He looked to see if I believed him, but I shrugged and said, 'That's nothing — I'll give you double for it.'

'Ah, maybe,' he retorted sceptically, 'it's easy to say things.'

'But I mean it, I've the money here.' I then started to count out coins from my sovereign purse. As he saw the gold spreading in a small heap on the table, his eyes goggled and he left us saying, 'I must fetch my old woman.'

When he'd gone my friend said, 'Quick, spread it all out, I think we may make a fair deal after all.' As he spoke, he swivelled round a movable hanging gas jet so that its light shone directly upon the spread out gold coins. We were ready by the time the landlord came back with an untidy old woman with red-rimmed eyes. She looked first at us, then at the jug, and lastly at the gleaming golden sovereigns. As she looked her husband muttered to her, 'I could buy a pony'. Still she stared, then she spoke suddenly, 'Oh please yourself,' and left the room without another word.

The landlord said, 'Well, throw another 'alf quid for luck guv'nor, and the old jug's yours.' Quickly I threw down another half-sovereign and then, picking up the jug, started to wrap it in the newspaper we had with us.

The landlord shouted excitedly, 'Aaf a mo', the boys must see this or they'll never believe me.' He rushed to the door and shouted down the passage, 'Hey, boys, come up here.' Almost at once six or eight rough-looking men stood at the door. For a second I wondered whether we were going to lose both jug and money! But the innkeeper said dramatically, 'Boys, I've bin 'an sold me old jug . . .' A long pause and then a roar, 'An' THERE'S THE BLOODY MONEY!'

I've never forgotten the vivid scene even after all these years. We, the two dealers with our backs to a small shuttered window, the round table covered with a dirty red tablecloth and the beautiful jug surrounded by twenty sovereigns and one half-sovereigns in gold. The swarthy, black moustached landlord, his cheeks red with excitement, his eyes gleaming, one hand resting on his hip, the other pointing at the table. The peering, unshaven faces at the door, the smell of beer, sawdust and wafts of shag tobacco, the atmosphere of avarice and high drama. It was almost an anti-climax to sell the jug afterwards to Captain Price for £95, although we were delighted.'

Part of the fun of collecting is 'the hunt'. I know of few millionaire collectors, but it cannot be much fun giving a blank cheque to a top dealer with orders to purchase twenty of the best Tobies. He may end up with one of the finest collections in the land, but it is a bit like giving the fox hunters the dead fox and telling them not to bother with the hunt! Toby hunting is fortunately much more humane. It is often more fun to travel hopefully than to arrive, and my favourite Toby Jug is usually the one that I have just bought, with the excitement of finding it fresh in my mind.

New collectors must read all that they can on the subject, visit museums and meet and talk to kindred collectors and dealers to build up a knowledge of the subject — there are always new stories, new ideas and new information. It is a good idea to build up a photographic album or a folder using articles from magazines, newspapers and auction catalogues.

It is something of a mistake to start collecting by buying a number of low priced jugs. It is far better to save and buy one good jug than plunge into a cheap collection, for if you buy wisely you will not regret it, you will enjoy the company of your Toby. If you should wish to sell at a later date, you will get your money back with interest. This is not so with the cheap and nasty Tobies, of which there are so many, they do not look particularly attractive and cannot really be resold, so think about this when you purchase.

In the antique ceramics field the usual advice regarding the quality of jugs is 'never buy damaged pieces'. This may have been true in the past when fine pieces were plentiful and less costly and it is true of modern pieces of fine porcelain, but it is particularly difficult to find Toby Jugs which do not have some element of damage about them. The prices that many damaged jugs fetch can be quite staggering, so don't expect every jug you collect to be perfect and do expect to get good prices even if your jug is damaged if and when you come to sell.

CHAPTER TWO
Who was Toby?

Oxford Concise Dictionary
Tope: To drink intoxicating liquor to excess esp. habitually hence, Toper (Toby)

The reader will initially be concerned with the origin of the Toby Jug and may expect some definitive answers as to why the Toby Jug came about and who first made the character in its original form, but tracing the early life of the Toby is not easy, as will become apparent throughout this book.

In assessing the age of a jug and its maker, the collector must learn something of 'the feel', the texture, the colours used in glazing and the weight and style of potting, rather than rely on makers' marks on the bottom of the jug. The collector must develop his own skills of judgement, and it is these individual skills which spice the debate as to the age of jugs, their maker and their value.

There are a number of suggestions as to which character inspired the production of the first 'Toby'.

In the eighteenth century the profession of the 'Footpad' was known as the 'Low Toby'. He was today's equivalent of the street mugger, and he was obviously not very well liked. The more romanticised figure of the same ilk is the Highwayman on horse-back, who was known as the 'High Toby'. While this is worth a mention it is unlikely that there is an association here with the character as we know him.

Some also see him as the Shakespearean character of the same name in Twelfth Night. Certainly the character is a drinking, foolhardy man, but a more viable claim is that he was one of two notorious drinkers of the late eighteenth century who were reputed to have drunk a great deal of 'Stingo', a strong British ale of the time. One such was Henry Elwes, a Yorkshireman, who died in 1761 having drunk an estimated 2000 gallons of the beer from a brown jug, and was nicknamed 'Toby Fillpot'. The other claim is accorded to Paul Parnel who was acknowledged for his drinking prowess in Gentleman's Magazine of 1810 for drinking 'out of a silver cup upwards of £9000 worth of Yorkshire Stingo, being remarkably attached to Stingo tipple of the homebrewed best quality'. At less than one pence per pint, this was really going some, but whatever the modesty of the Yorkshire drinker in assessing the drinking prowess of his fellow man, one may question the statistical accuracy of information gathered whilst 'under the influence'.

More convincing evidence as to the origins of the Toby Jug is found in the popularity of a mezzotint produced by Robert Dighton to accompany a song written in 1761 by the Rev. Francis Faulks — a humorous and very British adaptation of the Latin poem by Geranimo Amelto.

This song is presumably to be sung holding a pot of foaming ale, whilst the singer explains how the jug which he holds is made from the deceased body of Toby Fillpot, or 'Phillpot':

> **The Brown Jug**
> Dear Tom, this brown jug that now foams with mild ale
> (In which I will drink to sweet Nan of the Vale),
> Was once Toby Fillpot, a thirsty old soul,
> As e're drank a bottle or fathom'd a bowl;
> In boozing about 'twas his praise to excel,
> And among jolly Topers he bore off the bell.
> It chanced as in dog-days he sat at his ease
> In his flow'r-woven arbour as gay as you please,
> With a friend and a pipe puffing sorrows away
> And with honest old Stingo was soaking his clay
> His breath doors of life on a sudden were shut
> And he died full as big as a Dorchester butt.
> His body, when long in the ground it had lain,
> And time into clay had resolved it again,
> A potter found out in its covert so smug,
> And with part of fat Toby he form'd this brown jug
> Now sacred to friendship, and mirth, and mild ale,
> So here's to my lovely sweet Nan of the Vale.

Courtesy of the British Museum

The song thus gives us both the drinking man and the character. It is known that this print was very popular towards the end of the eighteenth century. Aside from characterising popularly known figures of the day, fictional characters representing the mood of the time (like John Bull and Toby Fillpot) were

This popular mezzotint from Deighton is thought to have been the inspiration behind the first British Toby Jug, 1761.

also developed and incorporated into British life and culture by means of the mezzotint.

This print was originally copied as 'sprigging' (a moulded decoration applied to the sides of various types of pottery) for brown salt-glazed stoneware, sometimes also referred to as Toby Jugs. This sprigging has been used by various potters including Doulton in the nineteenth century. The decoration has also been used for plaques and is found on Prattware jugs such as those marked 'Ferrybridge'. John Turner is thought to have produced the first mould of this print, which is a faithful representation, and can be seen in the museum at Spode's Pottery, Stoke-on-Trent.

From the song we can ascertain that the date, the style of clothes, the jug and the pipe are just about right to form a model for the first traditional Toby Jug. The poem and picture later appeared in a book of original poems and translations and it was also introduced into a comic opera, The Poor Soldier by John O'Keofe at Covent Garden in 1783. It became so famous that it was quoted in Parliament. It is around this date that we see the first real evidence of a Toby Jug proper, which we will come to later.

A point worth mentioning here is that jugs in the human form have been produced ever since man began making pottery, for instance the Greeks and Romans also produced them, but the peculiarity of the British Toby Jug is that it has become an institution resembling to the Toby of the print, in drinking pose. The reason for the Toby Jug becoming so named is that 'Toby' is given in the third line of the song, thus giving an appropriate name for this particular type of jug.

What were Toby Jugs used for?

It has been claimed that Toby Jugs were used to convey ale to tables in country taverns. The Ordinary nine to ten inch Toby is quite large and would hold about a quart of ale, but in fact, whilst they may be an adaptation of the Ordinary jugs of a similar size and shape, it is unlikely that they were ever viewed as being practical.

The original Toby Jug was possibly big enough to carry ale, but subsequent jugs, made towards the end of the eighteenth century and thereafter, such as the 'Hearty Good Fellow', were totally inappropriate for carrying any liquid; the neck being far too small to pour from, and the inside of the jugs being particularly difficult to clean. This hygiene aspect was all the more important in the mid-nineteenth century when cleanliness was realised to be a prime factor in the fight against the spread of disease. So much so, in fact, that pottery cow creamer jugs fell out of favour during the Great Cholera Epidemic of the 1850s. The Toby survived because it is unlikely that it was in use as a jug.

Although the original Toby Jug may possibly have served some practical purpose it can generally be taken that its function was subsequently nothing more than ornamental.

Americans often ask me, "What are these pitchers called?" I have to tell them, "They are Toby Jugs. You hang 'Pitchers' on the wall".

CHAPTER THREE

Who made the first Toby Jugs?

The early makers

Just who made the first Toby Jugs is a matter of conjecture. There were many potters in the Staffordshire potteries who in the last quarter of the eighteenth century could have produced the first Toby.

The three most commonly cited potters of the early jugs are **John Astbury** of Shelton (1688-1743), **Thomas Whieldon** of Fenton (1719-95) and **Ralph Wood I** of Burslem (1715-72), but there is no evidence that any of them made the first standard Toby Jug. It is important that we look briefly at why these potters could or could not have produced the first jugs before going on to look at the arguments for **John Wood**, **Ralph Wood II** and some other early potters as being among the first of the makers of the British Toby Jug which is so familiar to us all today.

We can establish the fact that the first potters of the British Toby Jug lived within the small area known as the Staffordshire Potteries. Identification of who did what in the eighteenth century is virtually impossible, not only because potters did not mark their work, but also because, in the narrow confines of the area in which they lived, potters often worked with one another and for one another, so it is difficult to distinguish between them. Indeed the potteries of that period can be seen as one interrelated family — they married each other's sisters, they pilfered one another's ideas, they went into business, they lent money and gave credit to one another — in fact they almost lived and worked as a single family, with all the quarrelling, feuding and imitating reminiscent of today's popular soap operas.

Toby Jugs which sell under the name of **Astbury** are most unlikely to be his, although the jugs known as the 'Fiddler and Midshipmite Group' ascribed to him are the most sought after. They appear to be early, but the type of pottery, modelling and glazing differ from what we might expect of Astbury. They are primitive in their style of potting, with some of the Astbury look about them, but no shards (broken pieces of pottery) were found at the excavation site of his pottery in Shelton which could justify the claim that he made Toby Jugs and they are unlikely to be the jugs which inspired continued production for the next two hundred years. Only one of this group of jugs is a drinking Toby in something of the form which we know today.

Fiddler £5000+.

Similar problems arise with **Whieldon** jugs, which can bring large sums at auction. These jugs are again quite primitively produced, but once more, there is no documentary evidence to substantiate Whieldon's status as an early potter of Toby Jugs. He never marked his wares and again, there were no broken shards at the excavation site of his pottery in Fenton which might indicate that he was producing them. These jugs do not look quite as primitive as the so called Astbury-type, and must be termed Whieldon-type if anything, though sometimes they are cited as being by **Twyford**. They can be identified by their mottled decoration and, quite often, by a relatively small jug held in Toby's hand which has a distinctive pear-shape. Other criteria for regarding a Toby as Whieldon is a step-base (referred to in detail later) and black staring eyes which can give the Toby a rather frightening appearance. It is quite possible that these jugs were being produced from c1765, but we shall probably never know who produced them, or precisely when.

It seems that there is some confusion as to the potting status of Astbury and Whieldon. Their names are often used generically, in association with the types of potting practice for which they are famous, rather than in the context of their being the definite producers of particular types of pottery. So it is quite inaccurate to term all eighteenth century Tobies with running mottled glazes as **Whieldon** or those with

Raised glass with B.T. on small jug. c1780-90.

Finely modelled raised glass c1780 possibly by R Wood.

Unknown maker. Note, large jug. c1800.

Sharp Face by Ralph Wood, c1785.

Long Face by Ralph Wood. c1785.

Ordinary Ralph Wood. c1780.

the primitively styled modelling of the 'Fiddler' and 'Midshipmite' type as **Astbury**.

The greatest misnomer relating to the popularly held conceptions of the early producers of Toby Jugs relates to **Ralph Wood I**, who is considered to have produced among the finest examples of the British Toby in a fashion which has laid the standard for all other potters of the past two centuries. Whilst it is true that these are among the best made in the eighteenth century and they do seem to follow the theme of Toby Fillpot of the song referred to previously, he can no longer, on current evidence, be regarded as the maker of these jugs. He worked for the Wedgwoods for the bulk of his career, certainly the last fourteen years, as a block cutter, signing his name on the saltglazed stoneware blocks which were used for making moulds. There is certainly no record of any pot-bank where Ralph Wood I could have produced figures and Toby Jugs during his life.

The confusion stems largely from the fact that 'R WOOD' and 'Ra Wood Burslem' appear on a number of late eighteenth century figures (and at least one Toby), and this is taken to be Ralph Wood I or his son of the same name, **Ralph Wood II**. Thus it has been thought that both men produced a range of high quality figures and Toby Jugs between them. It has also been thought that Ralph Wood I was responsible for the jugs which have running coloured glazes, an unglazed base, and the impressed name, 'R WOOD', whilst his son used fixed enamel glazes, glazed the base of his jugs and impressed his name 'Ra Wood Burslem'. But this simply cannot be true; the different methods of glazing were in use concurrently towards the end of the eighteenth century and Ralph Wood I could not really have produced his own Tobies and figures. We cannot therefore make the same distinction between father and son which has been popular in the past.

In fact, even Ralph Wood II is unlikely to have made a significant number of the figures and Toby Jugs popularly held to be his. He spent a number of years away from Burslem, in Bristol, (from 1774 to 1783) selling earthenware and glass, and when he did return he worked with **Enoch Wood**, his cousin, until around 1789. Only from then to his death in 1795 did he produce his own wares in his own pot-bank.

As if this confusion over the Ralph Woods were not enough, we have also to contend with the fact that **Ralph Wood III** took over his father's pot-bank from 1795 and 1801 until his death at the early age of 26. The only certainty over any of the Tobies attributed to the Ralph Woods is the one that bears the mould number '51' and the impressed mark 'R Wood Burslem' on the base. On current evidence this is likely to have been made between 1785 and 1801, by either Ralph Wood II or Ralph Wood III.

One other source relating to the Ralph Woods is the oft quoted invoice from Ralph Wood II to Thomas and John Wedgwood in 1783. This is for a group of figures (there are no Toby Jugs on the list), and since he had only recently returned from Bristol it must be that he was either selling his old stock or acting on behalf of his brother, John .

It seems that it was **John Wood Snr** (1743-97), the brother of Ralph Wood II who not only produced many of the major figures thought to be by Ralph Wood I and II, but also many of the Toby Jugs. He has been much neglected as a result of the fact that he did not mark his work, but he was a successful potter from around 1775 onwards and is known to have sold Toby Jugs in the year 1786 to a Mr John Edwards — four Toby Jugs 'coloured' for ten shillings and two 'china glaze' for four shillings. It is quite likely that he made Tobies before this date and he certainly has the most significant claim to producing the first of the standard British Tobies and variations on the theme, as he is known to have produced Tobies in the 1780s and we also know that he was reasonably successful — something which cannot be said of the Ralph Woods.

Because of the evidence that both men produced Toby Jugs, John Wood and Ralph Wood must share the honours for being the producers of erstwhile 'Ralph Wood Tobies', setting the standards for future potters, even though they may not have been the first. It may be better, therefore, to refer to those jugs with the Wood features as **Wood-type** rather than as 'Ralph Wood'.

The following is a list of jugs thought to be originated by the Woods':

The Ordinary Toby	Lord Howe or Man on a Barrel Toby (mould no 63)
The Ordinary Toby with right hand holding beaker (mould no 51)*	Prince Hal Toby
The Long Faced Ordinary Toby	The Sailor Toby (mould no 65)
The Sharp Faced Ordinary Toby	The Squire Toby
The Roman Nose Ordinary Toby	The Shield Toby
Marth Gunn Toby (mould no 13)**	The Tipsy Man Toby

There has been at least one Toby Jug (an all cream coloured Ordinary) recorded with a rebus of trees (a punning device for 'a wood') thought to be c1780-95. This device has appeared on a number of R. Wood figures including the figure of Apollo.

George Stoner a collector and dealer before the First World War had one of the raised glass Tobies holding a pipe in the right hand in place of the glass. One was sold at the Bute sale in 1996 for £1265/$2430.

Mould numbers are known to have been used by the Woods, but they could also have been used by other potters. The four numbers, 13, 51, 63 and 65 are commonly accepted as being mould numbers for Wood jugs, so the collector who finds similar numbers, about ¼" high impressed in the base of an early jug must ascertain from its quality whether he or she has found a Wood jug. The numbers appear only occasionally. The Martha Gunn No 13 is in my collection and may be a Wood jug.

The work of John and Ralph Wood II are so outstanding that the features which are common to them are unmistakable to the initiated. The fine modelling, the gaping unpainted mouth, the crow's feet at the sides of the eyes, and the general facial expression all have the same hint of quality about them, and once this is recognised by the collector, he should have no difficulty in picking one out from many, saying 'That's an early Wood Toby'. The face on some Ralph Wood jugs gives the impression of having a blind left eye. The colours are always subdued, never garish, such as found on Pratt Jugs. The brightest colour would be a blue coat.

Enoch Wood was the cousin of John and Ralph Wood, the latter of which he joined forces with upon his return to Burslem in 1783, and then formed a partnership with James Caldwell in 1790. Enoch was well known for his work in the late eighteenth century, and was known as 'The Father of the Potteries'. It is likely that he too made the conventional Toby and it is often felt that he produced the first versions of the 'George Whitfield' (often called 'The Nightwatchman') and 'The Drunken Parson' (or 'Doctor Johnson').

Over the years it has become apparent that some jugs are not as old as once thought, and what we have found to date ties in nicely with 'The Dighton Print' theory, for no mention can be found before publication, in 1761.

The first four are entries in John Wood's sale ledger:
Mention of first Toby Jug sold on 28 September 1785

John Wood supplied Mr John Edwards on 9 December 1785
      4 Toby Jugs coloured 10/-
      2 Toby Jugs china glaze 4/-

John Wood supplied Mr John Edwards on 8 March 1786
      10 Toby Jugs coloured £1-2-6d
      2 Toby Jugs enamelled 8/-

John Wood supplied Mr Saml. Dunbidden on 23 June 1786
      3 Toby Jugs 6/9d
      3 Toby Jugs sitting on barrel 6/9d
      (this would be Earl Howe mould no 63)

The four mould numbers impressed on R. Wood Tobies are:

* Where this jug has the impressed numerals 51, it always appears that the index finger on the hand holding the jug is raised apart from the other three.
**Having checked the height of the numbers on the Martha Gunn No 13, against the No 51 on 'The Raised Glass' marked Ra Wood, Burslem, I found them both ³⁄₁₆" high

No 13 Martha Gunn (The only one recorded in author's collection)

No 51 Ordinary with raised glass (very rare impressed, 'Ra Wood, Burslem'). One sold at the Bute sale, July 1996 for £6900/$14000 with buyers premium.

No 63 Earl Howe (Man on the Barrel)

No 65 Rodney's Sailor

If these numbers were used in numerical sequence and we know by the John Wood sales ledger that No. 63 was in production by 1786, it follows that Nos. 13 and 51 came before and No. 65 probably no later than 1787.

However, it transpires not to be quite as simple as that, for in the

Three 7" ordinaries, c1800.

John Wood sales ledger there is no mention of mould numbers, since they appeared to be used only in the works, and the ledger clerk was making up his own description for the items that were being sold.

There is no evidence that the numbers were used in numerical sequence and, to add to the confusion, the same figures in some instances were given different numbers, such as the 'Bust of Milton'. Numbers 81, 82, 90 can be found impressed on the base. 'Martha Gunn', 'Woman Mandolin Player' and 'Man Hurdy Gurdy Player' all have No. 13 impressed. The 'Man on the Barrel' and 'The Sailor' both have No. 65.

When one is looking at a ledger like John Woods, one must use the evidence with great caution, because the book is probably one of several being used at the same time. So one is only looking through a key hole and getting a restricted view.

The full picture could be very different, since documentary evidence on eighteenth century pottery sales is very scanty. The John Wood ledger gives a very valuable insight into what that particular factory sold, the prices they charged and so on. It does not prove that John Wood made the items, only that he sold them.

The ledger runs for 46 months between 30 May 1783 to the end of February 1787. During this period John's sales per month in sterling were (for figures plus Tobies):

1783	8 months	£0-5-5d
1784	12 months	nil
1785	12 months	£0-13-11d
1786	12 months	£2-5-2d
1787	2 months	£0-11-6d

This encourages the view that either John had other ledgers or he was not making the figures etc, and was selling them on someone else's behalf, since during the first two months of 1787 the ledger records that John was selling figures he bought from brother Ralph.

There is also an unitemised item on page 128 of the ledger, 20 October 1784. 'Toys from bro Ralph £1-17-1d' which suggests that Ralph may have been making them even earlier. He is in the directory as a potter from 1783 onwards in partnership with cousin Enoch Wood.

John's account shows that he had 20 customers for figures and of these nine ordered Toby Jugs. The first recorded Toby was sold on 28 September 1785, so, in the first 27 months of the ledger, only figures were sold. However once he started selling Tobies they were his best seller and from then to the end of the ledger, they made up 40% of his sales (of figures and Tobies). In fact, over the whole period Tobies sold better than any individual figure, with sales of 128 Toby Jugs.

The next best sellers were 'Stags' and 'Hinds' with sales of 43 each. But of course Stags were cheaper than Tobies, since he only charged 9d each for coloured glaze examples.

John Woods sales of Toby Jugs break down into:

8 enamel coloured (John called them enamelled)	6.250%
4 white (John called them china glaze)	3.125%
116 coloured glaze (John called them china coloured)	90.625%
	100.000%

Enamel coloured ware were far more expensive to make, but even so prices were not constant, for example:

Enamel coloured were 48d, 60d, 48d, 39d (average 48.75d)
White china glaze 12d (average 12d)
Coloured glaze 30d, 30d, 27d, 24d, 27d (average 27.6d)

It looks like a negotiated price, rather than a discount system. The enamelled colour price reflects the additional labour and firing costs, four times plain white, with the cost of the coloured glaze in between.

Toby Jugs by different potters can be so similar that it is worth noting some reasons for this. One is that skilled modellers who worked at the potteries were a rare commodity and worked for different potters on a self-employed basis, sometimes only for a number of days. It is not unreasonable to suppose that the modeller of the **Wood-typ**e Toby Jug may have taken his skills to a rival pottery who then produced something very similar. Another reason for a very great similarity between the work of different potters, not only in the eighteenth century but on to the present day, is that potters often used one another's moulds, buying and selling bankrupt stock, and so the same Toby may have been produced by more than one potter. After all, we must remember that the life-span of the average pottery in the Staffordshire area during the eighteenth century was only a few years and moulds were often sold on.

Many other potteries, have caught up on the popularity of the Toby Jug, producing their own in many different variations. **Pratt-type** jugs of this early period were made in quite large numbers. Pratt-type decoration can be noted for its distinctive colouring with yellows, blues and browns showing up brightly against a grey-blue earthenware. The most common feature of this type of decoration is the spotted pattern on many of the pieces, but it is unlikely that they were all made at the same pottery, the Pratt name being used generically.

We must not delude ourselves that all early Toby Jug production has come from Staffordshire. Many other potteries throughout Britain, like the **Swansea** pottery in Wales, made fine Toby Jugs and its wares were usually marked from c1780-1824. **Portobello** near Edinburgh, Scotland, made Tobies which can be identified by its use of a bright maroon enamel colour (from c1840). **Yorkshire** was also a prolific producer of Toby Jugs in the late eighteenth century and the first half of the nineteenth century (esp. Leeds).

Among the most common of the Tobies made in the traditional way are those by **Davenport**. He closely followed the eighteenth century craftsmen, both in technique and general characteristics, but he produced well into the nineteenth century and allowed himself to be influenced by prevailing fashions,

Davenport Ordinary. Dated and marked 1836.

Ordinary raised glass by Ralph Wood. c1780.

Pratt-type ordinary. Note, very small jug! c1790.

turning his talents to the production of brilliantly enamelled pottery and heavy gilding, far below the standards set by the Woods.

John Walton is another of these early potters who produced Tobies in the eighteenth century, but is largely considered to be a nineteenth century potter. Although his wares were made for lower classes and were mass produced in order to meet the limits of their purse, these Tobies were the best of their kind and had a certain originality about them. The jugs can sometimes be found with 'Walton' impressed on a raised ribbon on the base or on the back.

The excessive use of gilt and garish colours, as well as the loss of modelling definition in favour of mass production techniques, sets in from around 1840. There was a rapid deterioration in all artistic taste in England from the beginning of Queen Victoria's reign but it must not be taken from this that the later jugs like those of Davenport and Walton are of no value. They are still considered to be collectors' items. Generally, it is not until the twentieth century that the balance is redressed, with some very fine Toby Jugs being produced.

Other Early Potters

Palmer, Wilson and Neale are also known to be early potters of the Toby Jug and their jugs are of a very good quality, with 'Neale & Co' sometimes being found on the base. Neale was a London supplier of fine pottery who had much of his products made in Staffordshire, only of the best quality. Some of his Tobies are so similar to those taken to be by the Woods' that they could, at first glance, be easily be mistaken as such. Characteristics on some Neale & Co jugs are that they have a marbled base, the cheeks and nose are red and the mouth shows white teeth with some missing. Hair stubble is painted on, giving the impression of the face being unshaven, the eyebrows are bushy and these Tobies often have an overglazed red coat, or occassionally the coat is found in white. It is thought that the red and spotty face found on many Neale jugs, also the unshaveness was due to 'acne rosacea' which was said to be prevalent in the eighteenth century. Black cravats are sometimes found on Neal jugs.

Lakin and Poole of Burslem 1791-95. In keeping with all their Staffordshire wares, Lakin and Poole made very fine copies of 'The Hearty Good Fellow'.

Copeland and Garret 1833-47. This firm made Toby Jugs in the old Spode factory in Stoke-on-Trent, which is still in business today. *See also under 'Squat Toby' (Copeland Late Spode).*

As we will see later, the new assessment of the 'Fiddler' and 'Rodney' Jugs show that the most primitive and naive looking are not necessarily the oldest. In this category would come 'The Step Tobies', and creamware Tobies sitting on a 1⅜" high base. The latter holds a churchwarden's pipe in his right hand with the bowl held uppermost. This jug is very rare.

Another of the early jugs (*see right and colour picture on page 69*) is an amusing crude figure 7¾" high, whose modeller it seems had little knowledge of anatomy, as not only is the left hand almost twice the size of the right, but has five fingers and a thumb. An unsophisticated little chap who must have been quite astonished to have found himself in such grand surroundings of a London sale room (as I'm sure his maker would have been) where I purchased him. Captain R.K. Price shows two of these jugs in his book Nos 102 and 103. The jug is very light and has a ⅝" recessed base. Three Tobies of this type were sold at the Bute sale, July 1996 for £1955/$2000 with buyers premium.

The Toby without base (see page 38) might also be in this very early category, c1770, as along with 'The Bargeman' and 'The Thin Man'. This last jug is far less crude, in fact, it is quite sophisticated, with fine modelling and beautiful glaze and in all probability was a little later than the others, c1780.

Ordinary Toby. Note, right hand has five fingers.

Portobello ordinary. Note, thistle on small jug. c1830.

CHAPTER FOUR

The Ordinary Toby

This is the most common type of Toby Jug, the one which formed the original blueprint for the Tobies which are still in production today — and which, no doubt, will still be in production a hundred years from now.

The Ordinary Toby is usually 9"-10" high, depicting a seated figure clothed in eighteenth century style dress, the distinguishing feature being his tricorn hat. In the late eighteenth century this hat was known as a 'Kefenhuller' and was the standard male headgear throughout Europe and North America. Such hats were not commonly worn by sea captains, nor were they worn by Nelson and Napoleon as many people think (they wore bicorn hats). By and large the original tricorn hat was worn by the ordinary beer drinking man who enjoyed a pot of ale and a smoke.

The Ordinary Toby figure wears a long top-coat which would fall just below the knees when standing. Under this he wears a waistcoat and has a scarf, or 'stock', around his neck. He wears breeches down to knees and stockings underneath. His shoes are either fastened with buckles or tied with laces. On his left knee he balances a jug of ale which is usually full, and it is held by the left hand whilst the right supports it.

An interesting variation of this is an Ordinary Toby with the jug held in the right hand and balanced on the right knee instead of the other way round. These are rare, and it would be interesting to learn of any — but if you are working from a photograph it is as well to bear in mind that the print may have been reproduced in reverse. Two exceptions to this rule are 'The Farmer' and 'The Large Hands Coachman', although these two jugs are not strictly Ordinarys. There is one early Ordinary Toby recorded with the jug balanced on both knees in the centre. *(See also twentieth century Ralph Wood made by Kevin Francis Ceramics which has Toby Jug on right knee.)*

Two potteries made larger than usual figures of the Ordinary Toby. They were **Hollins** of Hanley 1794-1820 and **Shorter** of Stoke c.1940. The Hollins Toby is 12¼" high with a pipe down by the right leg. Shorter made a copy of the same jug with a black pipe which is not as attractive as the Hollins jug, being painted in harsh black, brown and yellow colours. The Shorter jug is marked, 'Shorter Made in England' or 'Genuine Staffordshire, hand painted, Shorter & Sons, England'.

Another variation on the Ordinary Toby, which is quite common, is a grey haired Toby, sitting with his head turned very slightly to the left. He can still be found wearing his detachable hat crown, which has a groove in it running from front to back and a yellow or red band around the hat brim. At the back of the jug is a nicely moulded chair-back and handle. These Tobies were first made around 1840-50 and continued to be produced into the twentieth century. The earlier versions tend to have softer colours with nice crisp modelling and hollow feet. The later reproductions have the small jug moulded into the body and are sometimes found with '1793' painted on front of base, although they are twentieth century Tobies.

The Ordinary Toby is so common that it is impossible to give values. One can only say that it is the variations on the Ordinary Toby theme which are most valuable to collectors, and, as such, the Ordinary tends to fetch slightly less on the market if it has no unusual features. An Ordinary variation by Ralph Wood is the drinking Toby with a glass raised to the mouth, held in the right hand. Because of this distinction, and the impressed name 'Ra Wood Burslem' with the mould number 51 on the base, this jug fetched £2600/$4000 at auction (Sothebys 1986). One very unusual Ordinary Toby, a 'Collier' type with the topers left arm outstretched holding a glass. Written on front of base is 'Joseph Marttain Burslam', sold at Sothebys 1989 for £1089/$1500.

Hollins 12¼", 1794-1820. *Shorter 12½", c1920.*
£1000/$1645

There are so many variants of the Ordinary Toby that we must not lose sight of him in the rest of this book. Nearly all the potters who made different characters of the Toby also made the Ordinary Toby which we only briefly mention here. It must be remembered that these variants, the family of which we concentrate on later, spring from his original.

An interesting Toby came into my possession recently. Its interest lies in the fact that it had its documentary history, written in 1891. It would have been nice to have known its story in the past one hundred years. I bought it from a young man in the Portobello Road in 1990 for £100/$150. It is a **Pearlware** Jug standing 9" high and has had a hard life. The hat has been completely replaced, it was cracked up the back, the coat and shoes being badly flaked, as is common with overglaze dark colours. The jug has a rust red chair and 'C' scroll handle, green waistcoat and yellow breeches. The most interesting fact is it does prove that this type of jug was made before 1827, a date one would put on a Toby of this type c1800-30, but not as the letter suggests, 1780. *See coloured picture on page 70.*

Ordinary Toby with its documentary manuscript.

The History of this Jug

It is supposed to be One Hundred years old from this date. viz: December 2nd. 1880,

It was for many years the property of Mr. Thomas Chapman of Bedford. who died in September 1827 after her death it became the property of her daughter Elizabeth, who had it in her possession for several years &, at her death left it to her brother Isaac. who ultimately made it a present, (as a relic to be kept in the family,) to his wife's niece. Eliza Covington in August. 1878.

The first named Mr. Chapman was. Eliza's Grand-mother her maiden name was Fanny Whale of Bedford Eliza Covington made it a present. to her niece. Annie Maria Covington. in February 1891. in whose possession it still remains this day. 16th of September 1891.

PURCHASED IN THE PORTOBELLO RD LONDON ON APRIL 7ᵗ 1990 FROM AN UNKNOWN MAN FOR £100 BY VIC SCHULER.

CHAPTER FIVE

Identifying the age of a Toby Jug

Identifying the age, quality, character and maker of a jug can be very difficult, and the collector will benefit a great deal from experience, gained from visiting appropriate museums and antiques shops as well as reading on the subject. The following indicates the major areas to watch out for when examining and identifying Toby Jugs.

The 'Feel'

A great deal can be learned from the 'feel' of a Toby Jug. Handling them and feeling the weight, warmth and texture of the jug can be very helpful. For instance, some old Tobies, which are made of a creamy light body, are very thinly potted and are very light in the hand. They can weigh as little as 1lb 11oz, against the weight of the average Toby which is around 2lbs 8oz.

It is reasonably safe to say that if an Ordinary Toby Jug of 9" to 10" high is noticeably light in the hand it will have been produced no later than c1800, as long as it is in keeping with the potting standards of the time. These Tobies are thinly potted earthenware and lack the bulk of clay, warming quickly in the hands. Porcelain and stoneware pottery are always heavier and colder to the touch.

The Glaze

It is also important to look at the glazing. Toby Jugs have been produced in a fascinating array of colours and three different methods of glazing are possible. In fact, unlike much of the mass-produced pottery of today, Toby Jugs of the eighteenth and nineteenth century possess an individuality about them which helps to make them such a fascinating subject for collection. Part of the responsibility for this lies with the artist who initially coloured the jug, much of the painting being very unprofessional, but nonetheless adding a uniqueness to the character. The following shows something about the types of glaze that were used.

Translucent Glaze

Up to c1780, translucent colour glazes were most commonly used for colouring the Toby. These colours were painted on by hand with a brush, but they were quite pale and this may have resulted in small patches on the 'biscuit' being missed. The problem was that after firing, when the glazes revealed their full colours, those omitted patches showed up all the more. This only occurs on translucent glaze jugs, so it is possible to use it as a means of identifying the age of a jug.

The only colours available to the potter for coloured glazes up to 1780 were:

Purple   obtained from manganese
Brown   obtained from manganese and iron
Green   obtained from copper
Blue   obtained from cobalt
Grey   obtained from cobalt
Yellow   obtained from ochre/iron

The shade of the colour was determined by the percentage of oxide used. These colours are beautifully pale and translucent, often running over their intended lines (for example the colour of the hat streaking down the side of the face) but still giving a very pleasing effect. This type of translucent colour glazing is associated with early Wood jugs, sometimes referred to as 'running glaze', although it is now known that translucent glazes and enamel colours were used concurrently. Because firing was often a 'hit or miss' affair, the glazes could quite easily be overdone, causing a running effect. Whereas today a jug might be thrown away if this happened, in the late eighteenth century, all of them would have been likely to be put up for sale.

Underglazing

Using this method, the metallic oxides were painted on to the 'biscuit' pottery and a lead glaze applied on top, instead of being mixed with the clear glaze as before. This resulted in a much thicker looking glaze with brighter, harsher colours. It was used from c1780-c1840 and generally became known as **Pratt- type** colours. The 'Pratt' colours are associated with **William Pratt** of Fenton (1780-99) who used this method of underglaze decoration.

From c1770 cobalt was often added to the glaze, giving a blue welling to the creases in the face, in between the fingers and on clothes etc. This today is referred to as **Pearlwar**e. Prior to this date, jugs were made of **creamware**.

Overglaze

This third type of decorating is where the whole palette of colours could be used. The jug was glazed and fired, painted over in enamel colours and fired again at a lower temperature in the 'muffle' oven. The problem with this method was that sometimes the colours tended to peel off, particularly the darker shades, the greatest offender being black. Flaking of colours is a common occurrence particularly on Staffordshire pottery.

In fact it became quite common to use both the underglaze and overglaze methods in conjunction with one another. For example, the collector will often find that where Toby's coat is blue, it is fired in underglaze with the remaining colours in overglaze.

Ordinary. Note, high base and pipe.

Crazing

Crazing, or 'craquelure' occurs when the glaze has contracted from the body of the jug. At first inspection there might not be any crazing visible to the naked eye, but inspection of the jug with an eyeglass will more often than not reveal it. If the crazing is minute, and the area bounded by the craze lines is less than " wide, it is an indication of an early jug (prior to c1820). The collector must remember though that crazing can be reproduced quite easily by modern potters.

Jugs with large brown crackle tend to be reproductions in which the crackle has been artificially coloured, usually with coffee stains or the like.

The Face

The colour of Toby's face varies from off-white to black, with jaundice colours, puce and brown between. Some eighteenth century jugs have cheeks which have large patches of manganese or brown on them. These faces often carry warts, pimples and even small pox sores (looking particularly gruesome, showing blood where picked).

A black spot appears on the cheek of one eighteenth century Toby in the author's possession and it is interesting to note that William Hogarth used to paint a black spot on the face of some characters in order to denote that he or she had contracted venereal disease!

The undeniable ugliness of some of these Tobies is not an indictment of their collectability; there is something fetching about the truthful representation of an eighteenth century drunken sot who seeks pleasure in beer in order to escape the harsh realities of life. The spots, scabs and 'splodges' are features which add to the necessary ugliness of the jug.

On the Ordinary Toby it is very rare to find a beard being worn, as beards were only fashionable throughout the seventeenth century and only came in vogue once more around the middle of the nineteenth century. So throughout the classic period of the Toby jug c1765-1840, men were clean shaven. The occasional Ordinary Toby sporting a beard is more likely to be a man who is unshaven. The 'Cavalier' and 'Falstaff' Tobies both have beards, but they are characters prior to the eighteenth century.

Very rare ordinary c1770. Note, high base overlap of feet and position of pipe. The feet are hollow as is the small jug.

In the Georgian period the lips and teeth tended not to be painted in at all because the fine definition in the modelling was thought to be sufficient. The Victorian jugs, being less finely modelled, had lips and teeth emphasised by red paint, giving a far less pleasing effect.

Gilding

During the nineteenth century the gold effect on ceramics was known as 'best gold', which was an amalgam of mercury and gold with a flux, hence its alternative name of 'mercuric gold'. It had a dull appearance and had to be burnished. With the very high cost of gold and the extra labour of hand burnishing, it was expensive. Over the years dusting has often rubbed away the gold, but in 1880, 'bright gold' was introduced. This was in a liquid form and was just brushed on, coming out of the oven bright and finished with no other work to do. The result was that the old 'soft gilt' look was replaced by this new, brassy, harsh look.

This is the gold to be seen on the Allerton Toby Jugs (1859-1942).

Hats/Detachable Crowns (sometimes referred to as measures, lids or stoppers)

It seems that all the Toby Jugs of the eighteenth and early nineteenth century were initially made with detachable hat crowns. It is unusual to find them still present now since they have been lost or damaged over time.

Pure black hats are rarely found on jugs before c1780 and it is interesting to note that on early jugs, the very edge of the brim can go quite yellow, showing that the black appearance is in fact dark brown. A coloured band around the hat brim is found on both eighteenth and nineteenth century jugs.

The Small Jug

A jug of beer is usually held in Toby's hand, with interesting variations in shape, size and decoration. The method of representing the beer froth is worth noting; a single flower appears as froth on the top of some jugs, (which is known to appear quite commonly as 'knobs' on Leeds teapot lids), an all-over pricking effect appears as froth on others, shredded clay (which looks like a pile of worms), or realistically, a bubble effect which is created in the clay. Sometimes this froth flows down the side of the jug.

In the eighteenth century the small jug was not usually decorated, indeed it appears that the **Wood-type** Ordinary Tobies had no decoration on them. One exception to this rule is 'The Windmill' painted on the small jug (see picture right). This is an English post mill painstakingly painted in miniature, making this Toby very unusual and rare. Probably made by **Neal and Co**, c1780.

The small jug must be a separate modelled item and not part of Toby's main body in order to qualify as an early Toby. When the jug held in the hand forms an integral part of the main body it can be taken as an indication that it was produced after c1840, since such methods were introduced then in order to simplify manufacture with front and back completed in two moulds.

Neal & Co, ordinary. Note, Windmill (Postmill) on small jug. c1790.

The Handles

Handles have an interesting variation in size, form and decoration. The most spectacular handle on the Ordinary Toby is the figurehead type on what is known as the 'Yorkshire' Toby. A **Wood-type** Ordinary model is even known to have a grinning monkey on the top of the handle. In 1989 **Kevin Francis Ceramics** started to have flamboyant handles made on their Toby Jugs. *See also Staffordshire Fine Ceramics.*

Modelling

Probably the single most important thing to look for on a Toby Jug is good modelling. The modelling should be crisp and vigorous on early jugs, the Toby having well defined teeth, eyelids, facial lines, buttons, buttonholes and laces. It should also show good definition on the neck scarf and waistcoat. As a mould is used, definition deteriorates, at which point is should no longer be used. Over use of a mould will soften the features.

Hollow Arms and Legs

Many early Ordinary Tobies have hollow feet which overlap the base (some jugs as much as ⅞"). If the feet are hollow, it is safe to say that the jug was produced before c1840. If the Toby is turned upside down, the hollowness of the feet can be detected through the overlap.

The feet and legs were always hollow on early jugs, but sometimes a sole was added to the shoes making the hollowness difficult to detect. It may be that the sole-less shoes were necessary to facilitate the firing process. Sometimes when soles have been added, and the arms do not have holes at the arm-pit, ¹⁄₁₆" diameter holes have been drilled into each arm and leg to let the gases escape. As yet we are not quite sure why the feet were left hollow.

Buckled Shoes

There is no truth in the rumour that the eighteenth century Tobies tend to have buckles on their shoes rather than laces. Although buckles went out of fashion in the early nineteenth century, it must be remembered that in the main they were used primarily by the gentry, the ordinary man would have laced his shoes.

Ordinary c1790.

The Tobacco Pipe

The presence of a pipe is usually a good sign, but it must be part of the original jug. Some Ordinary Victorian Tobies have a crudely modelled pipe lying along the right arm which is supporting the jug on the knee. Pipes were often an added feature, most commonly held in the right hand (which is supporting the bottom of the jug) or down by Toby's right leg, (not usually the left leg). Rarer still is a pipe situated between the legs or in the mouth, and this can often be used as an indication that the Toby is an early one. However, beware that the pipe is not a later addition!

Very rarely a Toby might be found where a pipe is held in the right hand, the bowl uppermost and the stem pointing downwards. On the 'Yorkshire' Tobies very elaborate serpentine style pipes are often found.

Barrel Between Feet

A small barrel or 'firkin' 1½" high may sometimes be found between the topers legs. These are found on eighteenth century jugs and usually not after c1800. One very rare Toby recorded had the barrel lying on its side with top of cask facing forward. It's auction price in 1989, was £500/$750.

The Base

Eighteenth century bases vary in thickness from ⅜" to 1⅝" – often with concave corners.

This base is the most common throughout all periods. Recess: approx ¼"

Eighteenth Century Base: Recess size is variable

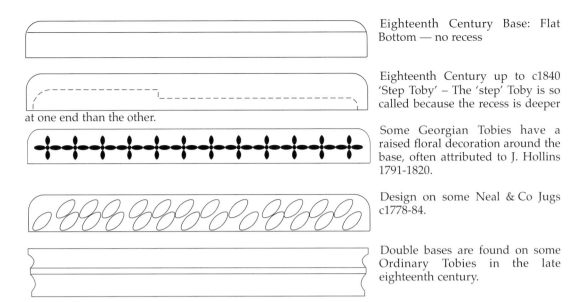

Eighteenth Century Base: Flat Bottom — no recess

Eighteenth Century up to c1840 'Step Toby' – The 'step' Toby is so called because the recess is deeper

at one end than the other.

Some Georgian Tobies have a raised floral decoration around the base, often attributed to J. Hollins 1791-1820.

Design on some Neal & Co Jugs c1778-84.

Double bases are found on some Ordinary Tobies in the late eighteenth century.

One could say (with tongue in cheek) that coupled with the Fiddler and the Viola Da Gamba Player, this 'Double Bass' Toby completes the musical string trio of the Toby Jugs.

The underside of the base of the eighteenth century coloured glaze Tobies are often completely unglazed or only glazed in part. It was probably thought unnecessary to glaze the bottom, but the glazing may have been omitted in order to prevent the pot sticking to the 'sagger base' during firing.

A painted line around the edge of the base appears on late eighteenth century enamelled Tobies such as those by **Neale & Co**. c1778-84 (contrary to popular belief that this was a nineteenth century innovation), but it is unlikely to be found on Wood jugs, nor on any with a translucent glaze.

A good way of testing the authenticity of what looks to be an old jug is to look through the top of the jug where the sides meet the base and check on any accumulation of grime and dirt. If the jug is old it will have accumulated over the years, even if it has been washed regularly (though few ever get a bath). Fakers do not usually think of this, so look for it when you are being sold 'the genuine article'. This might not appear to be very academic, but it works! Many early Tobies have their bases made of a box-like construction, being hollow in the middle.

.

CHAPTER SIX

The Different Toby Types

The Toby is obviously more than a simple representation of Toby Fillpot (or Phillpot), the traditional British character. He has come to represent a piece of British culture, and for this reason the Toby now represents many different characters, mainly by occupation. They are indeed a 'family' of characters and their depiction in terms of Toby Jugs has ensured that they will not be forgotten for their contribution to the development of the British way of life.

The characters of the Toby family are many and varied and one often wonders just how some of their names have been acquired. Only four of 'The Family' of eighteenth and nineteenth century Tobies have their names imprinted on the base; 'The Hearty Good Fellow', 'Lord Howe', 'Nelson' and 'Viscount Jarvis'.

The 'Snuff Taker', 'The Barrister' and 'Falstaff' among others, were given their names because they looked the part, indeed it may be considered to be an insult to the modeller if they had not been recognised as such.

Other names have been derived from the various objects which may be held in the hands, like a bottle, a book or a bell for instance. Others were given their names by early collectors, and rightly or wrongly, their names have stuck. Examples are 'The Nightwatchman', 'Prince Hal', 'The Tipsy Man', 'The Squire' and 'Earl Howe'.

It must be noted that the makers mentioned in the listings are those currently known, and there may be many other potters of particular types.

The Bargeman

This name was given by R.K. Price. This particular character is very rare, depicting a seated man with an anchor between his legs. He holds a flask in his left hand and a glass in his right and is dressed in the uniform of a waterman of the King's barge. He has a short jacket and baggy pantaloons, and on the sides of the rectangular mound on which the bargeman is sitting are cameos of the head of King George III surrounded by festoons.

This is a late eighteenth century jug, in coloured glazes. According to records only four exist: one in the possession of Captain Price, which was produced with a mottled mauve coat and which he thought had been made by **Whieldon**, one was on show at the Ideal Home Exhibition in 1976 (in the Pavilion, commemorating the bicentenary of the American War of Independence) and a third Bargeman sold at Christies Auction Rooms in 1977, coloured cream, green and manganese. It is primitively modelled with gruesome teeth, and stands 9¼" high. The fourth, again sold at Christies in July 1996 for £3680/$7360 with buyers premium, with restoration. The jug was from the Marquess of Bute's collection. *Colour picture on page 71.*

The Barrister

First produced by **Minton** of Stoke-on-Trent in 1873. It is 11¾" high, made in coloured majolicaware sometimes in polychrome colours also in Whieldon type running mottled colours or plain green or white. It shows a standing man with his hands in his trouser pockets. He wears a typical barrister's wig with a tricorn hat on top and a long gown with a cravat around his neck. The jug's handle appears as a long pig-tail reaching down to his waist, bound with ribbon and tied top and bottom with a bow. Hanging from his right waistcoat pocket is a watch fob seal.

There is a copy of this Toby in the Minton Museum. It is dated 1891-1912, described as 'eighteenth century Staffordshire salt glaze' and marked with the black printed globe of Mintons, England. A 'Barrister' sold in an 1984 auction for £1000/$1500. *Colour pictures on pages 98 and 99.*

This Toby was also made in an all over green glaze with the Minton date code stamp 3 (1903), as well as in majolica polychrome glazes, with a silver hat rim and hinged silver hat crown. The base also has a silver acanthus leaf pattern case. 'The Lady with the Fan' is treated in the same manner.

A companion to this is a female Toby which is similar in size and colouring, whose hair combines to form the handle of the jug. She is dressed in conventional Georgian clothes and has her left arm across her breast, holding a fan. *See under Female Tobies, 'Lady with the Fan' (see page 80).*

The Minton mark is found on a majolica jug 11¼" high, depicting a man standing, he is wearing a long coat down to the ground. His head is bald apart from hair at both sides. The left hand is behind his back holding a scroll of paper, the right hand is resting on his stomach. The very unusual feature about this jug is that the lip comes out of his chest.

To date, I've been unable to ascertain who this figure represents, a lawyer or politician? I'm aware of five of these jugs, but only one had the Minton mark. Joan Jones of the Minton Museum could find no record of this. This jug is also said to have been made at the **Sarreguenines** factory at Lorraine in France.

The Black Man Toby

This is a Toby Jug which was potted around 1850 at about the same time as the Staffordshire figures such as the 'Uncle Tom' and 'Little Abner' which are associated with the American Civil War. They were produced as a political gesture against the concept of slavery.

There are five different types of 'Black Man' Tobies. One is a standing man holding a jug in his left hand (moulded with the main part of the body). It is 9½" high and made in bright enamel colours. Copies may be found with a cobalt blue hat (which is unusual for a Toby), a yellow coat and striped hose. It has a stipple sponged base and handle (probably **Portobelloware**). Only two moulds are used in production for the front and back of the Toby. There are also models of this jug in which the figure takes on the appearance of a white man, and there are modern reproductions of this latter figure. *(See under 'Standing Man'.)*

The second type of 'Black Man' Toby is an Ordinary. This was made a little earlier, c1840.

A third type of 'Black Man' is a jug in brown pottery which has been painted in a blue/green enamel underglaze. The figure sits in the Ordinary fashion with the jug on his knee and he wears an unusually large tricorn hat. The lips are negroid so one can justifiably assume it to be a black man. It was made by **C. H. Brannam Ltd**. at Barnstaple, Devon c1900. It is usually marked 'Brannam Barnstaple' or 'Barum'.

These jugs have been recorded in sizes of 9" and 6" and one in an all over orange colour. One came into my hands quite recently in pale colours of green, blue, cream and yellow. The jug was 6" high and very poorly moulded, unlike most which are quite crisp. Barely legible on the underside of the base is inscribed 'Brannam, Barum'. Most of these jugs I have seen are quite deeply inscribed including the date 1900 or 1911. Incised lettering started in 1879 and the word 'Ltd' was added in 1913. **Value: £50-£100/$75-$150** *Colour picture on page 70.*

The Davenport pottery made a 'Black Man', *see under Crossed Leg Toby.*

C. H. Brannam Ltd also made three 9" high tobies of First World War leaders c1914-18: Marshall Foch (dark blue), Earl Kitchener (mauve/blue) and Admiral Jellicoe (dark blue), called Baron Toby Jugs series. *See also under Kevin Francis, Nelson Mandela, picture page 113.*

The Black Woman (or Negro Slave Toby)

This depicts a negress kneeling as at prayer, her hands together but chained at the wrists. She wears a pink coat, gold striped skirt, and wears a yellow bandanna with red wavy stripes on her head tied with an orange bow at her throat. Her back is formed into a 'crabstock' handle. The jug has a pewter hinged lid and is 11" high.

Mr Stephen Mullins of Chicago is the owner of this rare jug. The maker is as yet unknown, but was probably made in England or the USA c1850, in sympathy with the negro cause. Stephen Mullins thinks the figure represents a boy not a woman *(See picture on page 80).* One of these jugs was sold at Wintertons Auction Rooms, Lichfield, Staffordshire in January 1996 for £680/$1350 hammer price. This jug had no pewter lid. These are the only two recorded to date.

Bottle Toby

An unusual and very rare Toby which sold at Sotheby's, London, in July 1985 for **£2100/$3150**. The seated toper has a lop-sided stare and is wearing a slate-blue coat, brown waistcoat and ochre breeches. Between his legs he is holding a 5" high square shaped bottle. There are only two other known copies. One sold at Sotheby's Sussex in 1993 and the other can be seen in the Liverpool Museum. It is now thought that some might not be as old as first thought. This Toby, one can safely say, was made by the same potter who made the 'Wineskin', 'Reading Toby' and the 'Rodney Sailor' holding bottle. *Colour picture on page 65.*

Bottle and Goblet Toby

See under Yorkshire.

Bottle and Pipe Toby

See under Yorkshire.

The Cakes and Ale Toby

It is thought that this Toby was modelled on Shakespeare's *Twelfth Night* character, Sir Toby Belch, who had a fondness for cakes and ale. One Whieldon type miniature depicts Toby holding a glass in the right hand and a dish of cakes in the left. The Toby wears a green coat, yellow breeches and a tortoiseshell tricorn hat and is very rare.

Another model shows a seated gallant wearing a brown tricorn hat, yellow jacket and grey breeches, holding cakes and ale with a brown dog begging between his knees. The handle forms a knarled green bough on a square rock work base. It stands 10½" high, and was made c1785. **Value: over £300/$450.**

The Cavalier

A Cavalier was a supporter of King Charles I in the English Civil War of 1642-51.

'The Cavalier' sits in a chair with his left hand resting on his sword hilt and his right on the arm of the chair. This is one of the few Tobies in which the figure sports a beard and moustache. He wears a large brimmed hat which is swept up on the right-hand side in order to accommodate a feather. The jug was made c1900 in overglaze colours and is fairly common. **Value: over £75/$125.**

There is a jug in form the same as above, but in underglaze mottled colours. On the underside is crudely printed 'Pratt' Longport. 1837. There is no evidence that any potters of that name worked at Longport. They worked at Fenton, so this jug is obviously a fake.

The Coachman

A rare late eighteenth century Toby 7½" tall. The figure is sitting in a chair, wearing a pale manganese jacket, pale blue tinged waistcoat, yellow breeches, turquoise hose and kerchief and a brown tricorn hat. He is holding a jug in his left hand with a raised glass in his right. A rare Toby but it is hard to see how the name was derived. Sold at Sothebys in 1988 for £1100/$1650. *See picture page 71.*

The Collier

The Collier is the traditional British coal miner having a drink after his stint in the pit. He was renowned for his drinking habits which developed as a result of his dusty existence.

It is difficult to be precise about the prerequisites for 'The Collier'. Lord Mackintosh, a famed collector, suggested that he could be an Ordinary type Toby with a black or near black coat, but early Tobies with black coats are rare, and 'The Collier' may have any colour of coat. 'The Collier' should be so called because his face and hands are of a dark or dirty complexion. This dirtiness is often confused in auction rooms, the Tobies being catalogued as 'probably meant to be Negro'. The height is 10" and the base often has a raised floral pattern around it, the corners being concave.

These Tobies can be found with a small barrel standing between the Collier's feet, or he might be smoking a pipe held in his right hand. These jugs have been made both in coloured glazes and in enamel colours under a clear glaze. They were probably not made after 1800. **(Christies 1989 £1500/$2250).** *See colour picture page 71.*

The Convict

This is an Ordinary type of Toby wearing a brightly striped coat with broad arrows painted on it. These jugs are rare and Captain Price illustrated one in his book (see under Further Reading), though few 'broad arrows' can be discerned on his coat. However, the one illustrated above has a broad arrow decoration. **Value: over £700/$1050.** *Colour picture page 71.*

The Cross Legged Toby

There are various different types of these Tobies. All of them hold a jug to the chest in both hands, like a squirrel holding a nut. The most common is probably the jug which was first made by **Sampson Smith** of Longton (potting 1846-78), mould no 3584.

These jugs have a vacant look about the face with lips and teeth painted in red. The stockings are usually painted with a vertical chain pattern and stripes, and the jug which he holds has a floral pattern around it. **Value: over £50/$75.**

This Toby was also made by **William Kent** of Burslem in the last quarter of the nineteenth century and was still in the catalogue (No. 370) as late as 1962, listed as 'The Jolly Miller'. The jug is 8"-9" high, the figure sitting on a rocky mound, usually with a coat which is underglaze cobalt blue, overglaze red, or black. The hats are either red or black with a red or yellow band around the brim. They are often found with the hat crown still intact with a trilby type cleft. These Tobies are very common, but are more unusual if they have a blue willow pattern coat. Gold lustre Tobies of this model were made with no other decoration on them.

A very similar jug has been produced in two sizes, 8½" and 10½", but the head is turned slightly to the left and the hat is askew. The maker is unknown, but these are much more finely modelled jugs with a cobalt blue underglaze coat, yellow breeches, white stockings (with a vertical blue stripe and dots on them), black shoes with gilt buckles, a pink waistcoat, grey spotted neck scarf, a black tricorn hat with removable crown and yellow band round the brim. Again, Toby sits on a rocky mound with a red rustic handle at the back.

A copy of the smaller version of this can be found in the Brighton museum Willet collection. They date this c1820 and call it 'John Bull'. However, the bright gilding on the shoe buckles and the general style of the figure indicates that it was more likely to have been made at the end of the nineteenth century. Furthermore, John Bull was usually depicted with a curled brimmed shallow top hat, whereas this Toby has a tricorn. **Value: over £70/$115.** *See colour picture page 97.*

Davenport made a similar jug to this in which the hat has four corners to it instead of the usual three (the fourth being situated in the middle of the back of the brim). This Toby, a copy of which can be seen at the Stoke-on-Trent museum, has a blue coat, yellow breeches, a lattice pattern on the stockings and black shoes, the small jug is held by both hands by the right shoulder. In fact, this jug, which bears the Davenport mark, is so like the 'John Bull' type mentioned above that Davenport might well have been the maker of that jug too! Davenport also made this same four cornered hat in the likeness of a 'Black Man'.

The fourth type of 'Cross Legged' Toby is about 8" high and is much the same as the others in design, but tends to be rather moon-faced with the mouth, eyelids and arched eyebrows painted in rather than modelled and he has what seems to be straight lank hair down to his coat collar. The jug was shown in *The Connoisseur* magazine of March 1904, and was called 'Simple Simon', probably made c1890. It is sometimes referred to as 'Silly Billy' in relation to the street droll, Billy Barlow, well known in the East End of London in the early nineteenth century. **Value: over £150/$225.**

Dick Whittington

This jug is based in style on 'The Tithe Pig Parson' Jug but much smaller (only 5⅞" high). It shows a male figure presumably Dick Whittington holding a cat in both arms. This rare jug was sold at the Christies Bute Sale on 8 July 1996 for £1840/$3675 with buyers premium. A similar example was sold at Sotheby's on 17 May 1989.

Dolphin Handle Toby

Colour picture on page 69. Standing Toby 7" high with dolphin handle, c1820. The only one recorded.

The Drunken Parson (The Sinner or Doctor Johnson) c1800

The creation of this jug is attributed to **Enoch Wood**, although I've never seen or heard of one marked. It depicts a man sitting with a wine glass in his left hand and a jug in his right hand from which he intends to pour wine. He fails to achieve this, due to his drunkenness, and he looks to the right in a stupor with a leering expression on his face. His tricorn hat is askew on his head.

It is interesting to note that the Parson holds the glass at the foot, between the third and fourth fingers, giving the impression that he has five fingers as well as a thumb! He wears a black coat and white clerical cravat but when the coat is of any other colour this jug is known as 'The Unfrocked Parson'.

It may well be that the inspiration for the 'Drunken Parson' was a print by William Hogarth in *A Harlot's Progress* (scene 6) in which a glassy eyed cleric spills his 'Nants Brandy' (of Nantes?) out of a similar funnel shaped glass.

The base of the 'Drunken Parson' always has square sides and back with a rounded front, a feature which can be seen on 'The Nightwatchman' which is also attributed to Enoch Wood. The figure usually wears a full bottomed wig, known as 'The Physical' c1780. Less common, these jugs are found with the figure wearing the usual Toby type long straight collar length hair.

We know by looking at paintings of Doctor Johnson that he wore a 'physical' style wig. Should we then differentiate between 'The Doctor' and 'The Parson' by saying that Doctor Johnson wore 'The Physical' and 'The Parson' or 'The Sinner' the straight hair? This jug varies in height from around 7"-9¼". The Brighton Museum has one 'Doctor Johnson' marked on base 'T. Burnell, London'. An 'Unfrocked Parson', sold in 1991 at the highest recorded price for this type of Toby Jug reaching **£2800/$4200**. *Colour picture on page 71.*

'The Sinner' does not wear a clerical cravat or a physical wig, the first reference to this toby being called 'The Sinner' was, to my knowledge, by Capt R. K. Price in his book of 1922. Why 'The Sinner'? I don't know!

The Farmer

A traditional British character, much diminished in number by the onset of the agricultural and industrial revolutions in Britain at the turn of the eighteenth century. He is in the pose of an Ordinary Toby sitting on a wheatsheaf holding a foaming jug of ale on his right knee (an unusual feature but common to this character). He wears his hair with a fringe and his shoes have buckles on them. Note the unusual shape of the base *(see picture on page 71)*.

The jug was made in Musselburgh near Edinburgh c1820-30, and can be seen in the Royal Scottish Museum. **A rare jug. £1000/$1500+.**

Falstaff

Is a Shakespearian character who features in both *Henry VIII* and *The Merry Wives of Windsor*. He sits cross legged with a mug of ale in his right hand and his left arm sticks out, holding a club which forms the handle. This is another of those few jugs in which the figure has a moustache and beard. The jugs shown here are finely detailed and very crisply modelled, but certainly one of the finest of this kind to be found, standing 10" high in pale blue stoneware is the jug made by **Reed and Taylor** of Ferrybridge, Yorkshire (1843-50). It was registered on the 30 December 1845 and bears the diamond shape registration mark of 1845. There are two holes at the top of the hat to rivet a pewter-hinged lid. These lids are often missing and were probably not even fitted to most jugs. One has been recorded with a silver lid, hallmarked 1848, and there are others, made in white stoneware with pewter lids.

Jugs like this were made in brown salt glaze stoneware and more commonly in enamel polychrome colours later in the nineteenth century. In this century they were made in cream enamel. All the jugs seem to have the Greek key-pattern motif around the base.

There is another very similar Falstaff to be found in Majolicaware, by **Edward Steel** of Cannon Street, Hanley bearing the registration mark for 14 November 1883 though not all jugs are marked. They are about 9" high in which the figure sits with his left arm over the chair. In his right hand he holds a mug which he rests on his right knee and he sits cross legged wearing white breeches and hose, a green coat, a pale yellow shirt with blue facings and a blue tricorn hat – though these colours will vary.

There is something faintly reminiscent about the 'Prince Hal' jug here in the way the left arm comes out to form the handle. It is quite possible that all the foregoing 'Falstaff' jugs were based on 'The Prince Hal' jug which is sometimes referred to as 'The Falstaff' jug, and should be its correct name. **Value: £200/$300.** *Colour picture on page 97.*

Fiddler & Midshipmite Group

See Chapter Seven

King George III

It was brought to my attention quite recently, how much the well known brown salt-glazed stoneware Toby, with the hooked nose, who holds a jug of ale on his left knee and decorated with fish scales, is such a close likeness to King George III. So much so, that I think we should now refer to it as the George III Toby.

It is found in three sizes, 12", 11½" and 10¼". They are not always marked, but have been found inscribed: S & H Briddon and M. Knowles & Son, made in the mid nineteenth century, a finely moulded jug and valued at **£200/$400.**

There is one other 10" high, made in white porcelain, outlined in gold. There is no jug held in the left hand and right arm is stunted. Between the legs is filled in, giving no outline to the inside of the shins. The underside is unglazed. The one illustrated is the only one recorded to my knowledge, and the maker and year of manufacture is unknown as is its value.
Colour pictures on page 97.

Gesticulating Toby

This shows a conventional Toby 9¾" high, c1800 but with his arms held out in front, holding a jug on his right knee and a pipe. This was sold at the Bute sale in July 1996 for £2900/$5800 with buyers premium and to my knowledge, the only one recorded.

Mr Gladstone

William Gladstone (1809-98), was British Prime Minister four times. Sitting with his back to a tree trunk which forms the main body of the jug, he holds an axe which is resting between his legs. This refers to his enthusiasm for chopping down a 'tree a day'. The jug was made by **Sampson Smith** at Longton, c1870. Although it is not a particularly impressive piece of pottery it is very rare.

In 1948, at a disused part of the Sampson Smith pot bank in Longton, the old 'original' press moulds for this jug were found and a few reproductions made over a short run, but I have never seen the original or a reproduction of this jug. It is very similar to the 'Mr Pickwick' Toby made by **Sampson Smith. Value: over £75/$105.** *Colour pictures on pages 97 and 104.*

Two jugs made by Sampson Smith c1890; Left: Mr Pickwick, right: Mr Gladstone.

Lord Halsbury

Lord Halsbury was the First Earl of Hardinge Gifford, an eminent English Judge who was long time Lord Chancellor. He died in 1921. There is an ink and colour drawing by Carruthers Gould in the form of an ordinary Toby, but it is not recorded if the jug was ever potted.

Hands in Pockets Toby

A standing man, quite similar to 'The Snuff Taker', but both of his hands are thrust into his waistcoat pockets. The figure wears red breeches, blue coat and hose and a white waistcoat which is often lined with bright gilt and decorated with gilt dots and stars. He wears a black tricorn hat and has a silly grin on his face.

The jug stand 9¾" high, is quite common, and some models have the letter 'R' impressed on the bottom. Said to have been made at the Methvens Links pottery, Kirkaldy, Scotland c1880 (*see picture page 99*). There were reproductions of this jug made in the late 1980s.

Another standing man Toby with hands in pockets has a large pot belly, wearing a long coat down to the base, these come in varying colours, sometimes with a brown overglaze coat. Also in blue underglaze with elaborate gilding. They are found in various sizes. First made c1890 and still being made in 1990 (see picture right). 'The Barrister' and 'Motorist' also have both hands in pockets. **Value: £50/$85.**

The Hearty Good Fellow

Colour pictures on pages 71 and 72.

In the form of a man standing on a rustic mound (with 'Hearty Good Fellow' written on the front) and a tree trunk at his back, a branch of which forms the handle of the jug. The jug is quite large, at around 11" high. The figure holds the traditional jug in his right hand and a churchwarden clay pipe in his left. He is dressed in a long cut-away coat and colourful waistcoat and it is the variations to the decoration of the waistcoat which makes this jug so interesting. He wears knee breeches and white hose and buckled shoes. The completion of this attire is the tricorn hat with detachable crown, although more often than not this is missing.

Three Hearty Good Fellows: two on left wearing trousers c1790. Right, c1820 marked 'Walton' on back.

Other variations to look for in this Toby are:

1 Trousers in place of breeches and hose (these are early and very rare).
2 The stem of the pipe. This may be running along the arm, it may be pointing upward across his chest or it may be held in the left hand with the stem of the pipe in the mouth.
3 A large jug of foaming ale in the left hand instead of the pipe, balanced on the right fist, with the words 'Good Ale' written on the front.
4 Also bowl of pipe facing downwards. Another has a large pipe resting between legs.
5 A glass held in left hand in place of pipe.

The reason for calling this Toby Jug 'The Hearty Good Fellow' probably is that the potters **Lakin and Poole** of Burslem 1791-95, made models with this inscription on the front of the rocky base. One of these can be seen at the Stoke-on-Trent Museum, another in Captain R. K. Price's book (No.122), is mentioned but not shown. The Lakin and Poole jugs always appear to have 'Hearty Good Fellow' printed in black on a white cartouche with a black border, whereas the jugs made around 100 years later just have the name printed on the rocky base. **Value: over £500/$750.**

Although the jug has been produced for 200 years (**Tony Wood** potted one in 1983), there appears not to have been another one with the inscription 'Hearty Good Fellow' until 100 years later in around 1895, when **William Kent** produced them. **Value: £50/$75.**

Copies of this jug are found both marked and unmarked 'John Walton' 1818-35. A characteristic of the Walton jugs is that many of them balance the small jug on the right fist, whilst holding the jug by the handle in the left hand, i.e. they held the jug by the handle in the left hand and balanced it on the right fist. **Value: over £500/$750.**

A similar jug of ale, with a glass in the left hand in place of the usual pipe can be seen in the British Museum. Marked on the back, on a scroll, is the word 'Walton'.

There is one very rare H.G.F. marked 'Lakin & Poole' with the inscription on the front in a white cartouche with a black border 'With my jug in one hand and my pipe in the other', only one copy of this jug has been recorded. The impressed marks of **Turner** (c1780-86) also, **Neale and Co** (1778-84) are found on 'The Hearty Good Fellow'.

In twentieth century reproductions the figure is squatter and fuller in the face than the earlier jugs. Varying inscriptions have also been noted on the small jugs, such as 'Stingo', 'Good Ale', 'Success to our wooden walls' and 'Peace and Prosperity'.

One early (c1820) H.G.F. stands only 9" high, the figure itself being only 7¼" and no name on the base.

One has been recorded marked on base '1809', presumably the date of potting and another marked 'W' thought to be Enoch Wood.

The jug in my possession wears a brown coat, yellow waistcoat with black buttons, shoes and hat. The breeches are a mottled blue. The jug is quite crudely potted and holds no pipe or glass in the right hand.

Captain Price shows a similar jug in his book (No 96), which has a white coat mottled with blue and orange. The above two tobies are the only ones recorded. **£500/$750+.**

This Toby has also been referred to as 'The Old English Gentleman', maybe an early one had this inscription, but so far has not turned up. Another rare copy of this jug has 'Hearty Good Fellow' written down the length of the handle and on the small jug 'Stingo'. It is worth noting that on all written inscriptions on eighteenth and early nineteenth century Staffordshire pottery, the letters are finished with a serif. Without the serif they are reproductions!

See also under Vic Schuler Tobies and Twentieth Century Tobies.

Lord Howe (Man on the Barrel)

Colour picture on page 72.

Sometimes known as 'Admiral Lord Howe', 'Earl Howe' and 'The Man on the Barrel', this latter I consider to be the original and correct name.

A rare jug most probably first made by **John Wood**, who in 1786 billed one Samuel Dunbibben for three Toby Jugs sitting on a barrel for six shillings and ninepence (34p).

This must have been the Earl Howe jug, as there is no record of a Toby sitting on a barrel before this date.

One has been recorded as having 'Lord Hou' inscribed on the base. But so too has the 'Rodney Sailor', in fact two of these latter jugs are known with 'Lord Hou' inscribed on base. This jug always looks like a sailor, which is more than can be said about 'The Man on the Barrel'. I cannot recall one dressed as a sailor, and why a dog under his right foot? Not something I would have thought associated with the sea.

'Man on the Barrel' (Lord Howe) holding plug of tobacco in right hand, c1790. £2500/$4250.

It is surprising over the years how inconsistent dealers and collectors have been about the correct name for this jug. In the John Wood ledger of 1786 they are 'Toby Jugs sitting on barrel'; Frank Falkner *The Work of the Ralph Woods*, 1912, 'Lord Howe'; Cyril Andrade (early English pottery dealer) in *The Connoisseur* of April 1918 as 'The Publican'; Capt. R. K. Price had eight of these jugs and in his book of 1922 refers to them by the original name 'The Man on the Barrel'; Herbert Read in his book *Staffordshire Pottery Figures* (1929) calls it 'A Sailor Seated on a Barrel'; Edward Wenham in *Toby Jugs* (1947) calls it 'The Man on the Barrel' or 'Lord Vernon' and Bernard Hughes in *Georgian Toby Jugs* (1949) 'Admiral Lord Howe'.

Although 'The Man on the Barrel' is probably the correct name, for the past 40 years it has been called Lord or Earl Howe and probably this name will stick, but I must say this Toby does not remotely look like contemporary pictrues of Lord Howe.

Richard Howe lived from 1726-99 and as Admiral of the Fleet 'destroyed' Cherbourg in 1758 and won a famous victory over the French at Brest in 1794. At the end of the eighteenth century conditions in the Royal Navy became so bad that in 1797 squadrons stationed at Spithead (off Portsmouth) mutinied. The men's demands were met after a one week strike, the dispute being settled by the one officer they trusted, Howe. He rowed from ship to ship carrying letters of pardon from George III and was affectionately known by his men as 'Black Dick'. Why such a colour should be attributed to him is not known but it may indicate something about the way he dressed.

The jug shows Lord Howe sitting on a barrel wearing a tricorn hat clutching a jug of foaming ale with both hands. Under his right leg, which is slightly raised, is a King Charles Spaniel though some models are known in which this is missing. Resting on the barrel by the figure's left leg is a churchwarden pipe which again is sometimes omitted.

In the Liverpool Museum there can be seen an 'Earl Howe', which is all over green with a metallic lustrous glaze, probably c1820. The jug is minus the pipe by the figure's leg and stands 9" high. The base is unglazed. Only two of these Tobies are recorded. Another one, pictured on the previous page, shows a plug of tobacco held in the right hand. The jug handle forms a bunch of rushes tied with a rope on some jugs, but sometimes it is a plain 'C' scroll handle. The height of the jug varies from 9" to 10", some with a Wood mould number '63' impressed on the base. One is recorded in an allover ochre-glaze.

In June 1987 and in May 1990 the jug was sold in auction and on both occasions the hammer price was **£5000/$7500**.

A very nice reproduction was made by **Wood and Sons** in the late 1970s. *See under Wood and Sons, Twentieth Century Makers and Beswick 'Man Sitting on Barrel'.*

The Hunchback Toby

Colour picture on page 99.

Quite a common jug 9" high along with two smaller sizes. A sitting hunchbacked figure wearing a pale green or blue coat, red waistcoat, yellow breeches, pale blue stockings, black shoes and Tricorn hat. His hair is worn with a pig tail at back tied with a black ribbon. The figure sits on a square green base brushed with brown. In his left hand he holds a six-sided glass and in his right a jug resting on his right knee. This is moulded into main body and marked on the underside of the base, in black, is the number 289 and a stamp in red (Made in England), but unmarked this Toby was probably made early this century. Stafford-shire pottery unknown. Although a poorly modelled jug, it is interesting that jug and glass are reversed in the hands as found on Ordinary Tobies. **£50/$75+.**

John Bull

Colour picture on page 99.

He is sometimes called 'The Landlord' or 'The Rent Collector' but the original John Bull (1523-1628) was an English musician who is believed to have written the earliest version of our national anthem. In the context of the Toby Jug he is more of a bluff, good humoured, yet determined figure who personifies the characteristics of the English nation. This character was in fact created by John Arbuthnot in 1712.

He is depicted on transfer printed creamware jugs made during the last decade of the eighteenth century and also in the form of Pratt type jugs produced 20 years later. On these he is known as 'Boney and John Bull'.

The Tobies show John Bull as a sitting figure with a sheet of written paper in his left hand headed 'account' (sometimes omitted) and a bag of money in his right. He wears knee length boots, blue coat and black shallow top hat. John Bull was much popularised by Punch in the nineteenth century.

William Kent was possibly the sole maker of this jug, one being shown in his 1962 catalogue. It was first registered on 4 October 1890 by a Mr Gullic, making a search at the public records office.

This man's name appeared right through the year 1890, and it may be that he was a registration agent working for a number of potteries at the time. The registration number 153475 incised on the base indicates the year 1890.

John Bull by William Kent, c1900.

This Toby is very common, but less so the variation with multi-coloured coats, such as those with a floral or star-studded decoration in subdued colours. Their value is usually twice that of the others. £50/$75+.

See also under Bairstow Manor Pottery in the Twentieth Century Potters chapter.

The Landlord

Colour pictures on page 97 and 98.

This Toby is also known as 'The Publican' and was made c1850-60. It shows a man sitting astride a barrel which is marked on the front:

HOME
BREWED
ALE
1

One of these Tobies has marked on the base S. Smith, 1854. These jugs have Hat Crowns (covers) which are nearly always missing. This hat is decorated with vine leaves and five bunches of grapes. This jug has been found with 'S 1815' printed on the bottom in rust red ⁵⁄₁₆" high numerals under the glaze. Sampson Smith started potting c1846, so if this date is the year of potting, it could mean that moulds were purchased from a other potter before new ones were made at a later date.

'The Landlord' wears a blue underglazed coat but other items of clothing vary in colour and decoration and are in overglaze colours. Around his head is a garland of grapes and vine leaves and his grey hair is worn down to his shoulders. He holds a floral decorated jug in his left hand and a glass in the other. The base forms a grassy mound with a crabstock handle at the back. The jug comes in three sizes, 9", 11" and 12". **£200/$300+. with hat.**

These jugs have hat covers which are invariably missing. This hat is decorated with vine leaves and bunches of grapes. This self same jug may be found with the raised letters on the front of the barrel, replacing the words 'Home Brewed Ale' with

and on another

These two jugs were found recently by Judy Oliver and Cyril Wickham. What is interesting is that they are marked on the underside 'Wetley China' and a large 'S Made in England'.

We must note also that the name Sampson Smith sometimes in raised letters was used on the bottom of some of his jugs, for example 'The Crossed Legs Toby' and on 'The Landlord Jug'. 'Home Brewed Ale' is in raised letters also, although this might be only coincidental.

Sampson Smith died on 26 December 1878 aged 65. The pottery continued under his name until 1888 when Messrs Adderley & Tams took over until 1912. Between 1912 and 1918 the pot bank was owned by John Adderley and W. H. Davies. Around 1948, Barker Brothers Limited became the owners, and later Wetley China of Longton took over and were still in business in 1963. It must be noted that Shorter, at some time acquired some Sampson Smith moulds as they produced a jug entitled 'Parson John' which is in fact identical to Sampson Smith's 'Pickwick' Toby.

Doulton of Lambeth (better known since 1913 as Royal Doulton) made brown saltglaze Tobies of men on barrels between 1870 and 1880, one type bearing the mark 'XXX'.

Large Hands Toby *(See also under 'Coachman')*

Colour picture on page 72.
An Ordinary Toby, sitting, with unusually large and ungainly arms and hands. In his left hand he holds a glass and in his right a jug, which is balanced on his right knee, unusual for an Ordinary Toby. It is usually yellow with incised rings round the neck. This character has a smiling almost girlish face and a pigtail at the back of his head and wears a coat which is invariably a reddy brown. The head and hat are rather large and the jug usually has its bulbous detachable hat crown intact. The handle is of the rustic type.

These jugs come in different sizes, from 7" to 11" high. They are glazed in bright enamel colours and were once thought to be rare, even unique. However, this has proved to be a misnomer, as there are a number of these jugs around.

One jug although not strictly an Ordinary Toby, appears to be the only one quite similar, with the small jug on right knee and glass in left. One recorded has the small jug in silver lustre. This Toby is sometimes referred to as 'The Coachman', the reason not being very apparent. **Value: over £500/$825..**

John Liston 1776-1846

John Liston was a popular comedy actor, said to be the greatest of his time, and in fact was the first comedian to command a salary greater than that of a tradesman. There are a number of face (character) jugs of Liston, portraying Paul Pry, the central character in a play of the same name by John Pool, written in 1825.

I know of two Tobies, one 6½" high, the other around 4". Both are quite rare and made c1825. The mark of Enoch Wood is said to be on one of these. **£300/$450+.**

Long Face Toby, Sharp Face Toby and Roman Nose Toby (the Wood variations)

Colour picture on page 72.
'Long Face' is an Ordinary type Toby, but with a longer face (*colour picture page 72*). It is difficult to describe, so it is best to compare with a photograph along side an Ordinary (*see page 68*). Most 'Long Face' Tobies are of the drinking type (glass raised in the right hand) and all of them are thought to be by the Woods.

There is also the non-drinking 'Long Face', one of which may be found with 'Ale' printed on the small jug. This is unlikely to be made by Ralph Wood. The 'Sharp Face' Toby has a chubby face, but with the thin hooked nose. This jug is the raised glass type likely to be made by Ralph Wood. It is not to be confused with the Roman Nose Toby (*colour picture page 74*) which is the Ralph Wood Toby without the shield. All these types are rare and valuable.

Often the Long Face is taller, around 11", but some models are only 10⅜". **These jugs can be valued at over £2000/$3000.**

Loving Cup or Two Handled Toby

Although this is made in the form of a loving cup, owing to it possessing two handles, it is still a jug as it has two pouring lips. It is modelled in the form of a 'Squat Toby', both sides showing the front only. Painted in overglaze colours which tend to flake quite badly, wearing a red coat, black hat and shoes, made c1900 and later. **£50/$75+.** *Colour picture on page 76.*

Man in a Barrel

Colour picture on page 97.
Showing an angry man with his tongue out. 14" high with impressed mark

W&R Wayte & Ridge c1864
L
Wittman & Roth. Importers of London
c1870-96

Man in a Barrel by Wayte & Ridge, c1864.

Man on Barrel

There are a number of Tobies showing a man on a barrel, one of which shows a barrel on its side. The slightly built man's legs are over the end of the barrel, and holds a glass in his left hand and bottle in his right. The coat is draped over the barrel. This jug is believed to be **Portobello**, and one is shown in the John Bedford book *Toby Jugs* on page 39. I've only come across one other for sale which was in 1993 at an asking price of **£800/$1200.**

A very rare Sailor Toby sitting astride a barrel was sold at the Christies Bute sale in July 1996. The figure is smoking a pipe held in the left hand and holding a mug of ale in his right, is 6" high and was made c1800. The handle was a replacement and it had other restoration, but still realised £2530/$5000 with buyers premium.

See 'The Landlord', 'The Publican', 'The Postboy' and 'Earl Howe', all of which are topers which sit on a barrel. *See also under Doulton and Fielding in Twentieth Century section.*

Merry Christmas

This is not strictly a Toby Jug as it is only waist high and depicts a man holding a Game Pie dish at the top of which is a hare or rabbit. These come in two sizes, 8" and 6". Around the base in raised gilt letters is 'Merry Christmas'. The man is wearing a tricorn hat, around which is vine leaves and sports a moustache and beard. His hair hangs down over the collar of his underglaze Cobalt Blue coat.

This Jug is so similar to the 'Home Brewed Ale' Toby made by Sampson Smith that I feel it most probably was made by him c1855. The general style, the tricorn hat with vine leaves, the raised lettering, the Cobalt Blue coat, the style of the hair and the shape of the handle is the same. He also has a chevron painted waistcoat. *Colour picture on page 97.*

The Mystery Toby (or Open Mouthed Toby)

At first glance this appears to be a 9¾" high Ordinary type Toby jug with hollow feet. But this is not so, as the mouth is open, leaving a ⅜" hole into the body of the jug. There is also a 1¾" hole in the base with no handle. Both these holes where made at the time of manufacture as the sides are glazed over. There was never a handle fitted as there are no marks where it might have been, but there are graffiti marks under the glaze, as if the potter had done this to show that no handle had been fitted (*see picture below and colour picture on page 97*).

It is decorated in underglaze colours, under a **Pearlware** glaze with the coat in pink lustre, which in itself is rare. It was probably made in Sunderland.

With reference to the hole in the base, J. Shaw of Tunstall 'Burlingtonware' 1931-63, made a Toby lamp with the same 1¾" diameter hole. These Toby lamps have a dome shaped,

Pink Lustre Toby with open mouth, made without handle, c1830.

filled-in tricorn hat which held the light fitting, and secured with a spanner through the base hole. If a light fitting was fixed onto the loose hat crown (which is now missing), there would be no need for a hole in the base, but this arrangement would be impracticable since it would topple over. Apart from this, the jug dates from c1830, pre-electricity.

It has been suggested that it sits over a candle, I can feel no point in that (even if the seated figure could!). I thought that maybe a rubber tube was fitted with a bulb at one end, and when squeezed it would spew out liquid through the mouth as a joke.

To date, it remains *A Mystery Toby*.

Napoleon

Made in brown saltglaze stoneware by **Doulton and Watts** at Lambeth, c1825. It shows Napoleon standing, his left hand thrust into his waistcoat in characteristic pose whilst his right hand holds a small telescope. Considering it is said that more figures were made in England during the nineteenth century of Napoleon than of anyone else, strange how few Toby Jugs there appear to be. **Value: £250/$325.**

Nelson

Colour picture on page 99.

Viscount Horatio Nelson (1758-1805) died at the Battle of Trafalgar aboard his flagship 'The Victory'. This Toby shows Nelson standing on a rocky mound with the word 'Nelson' printed on it and this mound rises up Nelson's back to form a handle. At his back is a black cannon barrel.

One version of this is an enamel jug painted in a very pleasant mottled brown with a yellow waistcoat and red breeches. Although the figure can be found with the uniform navy blue colours, it is more often than not painted with a yellow waistcoat and red breeches. There does not seem to be any justifiable reason for this, for we would expect naval men to be wearing navy blue.

There is a jug of Nelson in the Brighton Museum, taken to be mid-nineteenth century, but it is highly improbable that any jugs were made before 1866, the date of the completion of Nelson's column in Trafalgar Square, London. It was at this time that there was renewed interest in the sea hero.

Parr and Kent first made this Nelson jug in the 1840s it is said. **William Kent** had them in all his catalogues as late as 1955. **Value: £50/$75**

The **Gladstone Pottery** of Longton was potting reproductions as late as 1975 where they probably acquired the moulds from William Kent. The first ones had no name on the front of the rocky base. All the later reproductions had 'Nelson'. This jug is common, but rarer are the ones without the name. This Nelson jug was also made in all over copper lustre.

Nelson with silver and gold lustre and enamel colours.

Other examples of Nelson jugs have been found including one made in blue and white underglaze, 11¾" high, made in the late nineteenth century or early twentieth. 'The Staffordshire Figure Co' produced one in 1995, standing 11½" high and retailed at £13, and Bairstow Manor Pottery using Kent moulds in 1997.

Nightwatchman

See under George Whitfield Toby.

No Base Toby

Colour picture on page 65.

A very rare eighteenth century Toby. Free standing, the feet are hollow up to the knees. The coat is green coloured glaze, the face and front of coat are splashed in manganese, most of the jug is in an unglazed buff colour. The jug stands 7" high.

The only other known jugs of this type recorded is shown in R.K. Price's book (Fig 104), which shows an

almost identical Toby, except that the figure's right hand is on left breast; where as the one illustrated the right hand is on right knee. Strangely both hats appear to have been cut down, but this is not so as the rim is glazed over, so probably there was a hat that lifted off. One other was sold at Christies, King Street, in 1988 for **£2800/$4200**. This had a pipe lying across knees.

See also 'The Tipsy Man' which has no base.

One Armed Toby

The 'One Armed Toby' was never designed as such, there being no record of Tobies actually modelled with one arm or hand apart from 'Nelson'. A number of early Tobies did however suffer the loss of an arm or a hand before the gloss firing process. This has thus given the impression that the 'One Armed Toby' was intentionally made this way with the glaze running over the broken limb. In spite of this the effect is not totally realistic because one would expect that the arm of the Toby's sleeve would be pinned back or rolled up. One might also expect there to be a hook or something where the stub of the arm comes out of the sleeve.

For a number of collectors these are still acceptable Tobies though, and they can sell for quite large amounts in auctions. Although in essence they are flawed pieces, the early jugs have good modelling in every other respect, thus maintaining its value on the collector's market.

Paternal Toby *(the name is mine)*

This is an Ordinary Toby type, but standing on his left knee is a small boy 3¼" high wearing a black tricorn hat. Also on his knee is a child's rattle. In Toby's right hand is a book from which one would think he is reading to the child. The coat and breeches are blue, tricorn hat and shoes black, vertical blue stripped stockings. The whole stands on a coloured splashed base with a blue dashed handle. The jug stands 10⅝" high, heavy and crudely modelled probably twentieth century and continental. It has a thick white tin type glaze. **£150/$225.** *See under Yorkshire.*

Mr Pickwick

Colour picture on page 97.

The main character of Charles Dickens' first novel *Pickwick Papers*, published in 1836.

It shows Mr Pickwick standing with his right hand raised, wearing a beaver hat and spectacles. He stands on a rustic base on which is written 'Mr Pickwick'. This is quite a common jug, made by **William Kent,** probably first made in the last decade of the nineteenth century and was still in his catalogue in 1960 listed as No. 391, 7½" high. **£100/$150+.**

There is a much rarer 'Pickwick Jug' showing him sitting on a tree stump. The figure wearing spectacles, has black boots halfway up his shins, he holds a glass in his left hand, whilst a spotty handkerchief is in his right. Only four of these jugs seem to be on record to date.

One was sold at Christies on 18 March, 1957. This jug was 8½" high and was wearing a yellow waistcoat, blue coat and pink breeches. It was marked 'Sampson Smith. 1851. Longton', in raised capitals.

The second can be seen as Plate 82 in Reginald Haggers book *Staffordshire Chimney Ornaments*. This figure is wearing a lattice pattern waistcoat.

The third is in my possession, it is 7" high with a black coat, white breeches and waistcoat and, in addition to his spectacles around his neck, hangs a monocle on a gold cord.

The final jug was once owned by Diana Ginns. This also had a blue coat.

It is worth noting that many Sampson Smith pieces, when marked, all seem to have the date 1851, but these 'Pickwick' jugs were probably made c1875.

Left: Mr Pickwick by Sampson Smith, c1875; Right: William Kent c1875 or later.

In 1939 **Shorter & Son** made an identical jug which was entitled 'Parson John' probably made from the same Sampson Smith moulds. This jug is very similar to the 'Gladstone' Toby but minus the axe.

The Postboy

Colour picture on page 98.
A name given to a Toby, depicting a man sitting astride a barrel. He has a stern, staring face and a black moustache with dots for eyebrows. He seems to be wearing a postman's hat of the style worn around 1890 (when the jug was probably made). The arms and legs are an integral part of the body, so only two moulds were used apart from the handle. He holds a glass in his right hand and a bottle in his left. It is a poorly modelled jug but is quite rare, and a picture of it appeared in *The Connoisseur* in March 1904. No jug has been recorded apart from this.

The Postillion

Colour picture on page 72.
A postillion was the coach driver who used to guide a group of horses from the saddle, on the near side of the leading horse, rather than from the top of the coach. This is very like an Ordinary Toby, except that the hat is a bicorn rather than a tricorn and he wears top boots rather than the usual stockings.

The seated figure carries a jug of foaming ale in his left hand and a glass in his right (although one has been recorded in which the vessels were opposite). They were made in various colours, and their height is around 7¼". The figure has rather staring eyes with a distinctive pot belly protruding from his coat. Sold Sothebys, 1988 £3800/$5700.

The Prince Hal Jug

Colour picture on page 72.
Sometimes known as the 'King Hal' jug. It is a striking jug, said to represent Sir Toby Belch from *Twelfth Night*, or George IV who when Prince of Wales, masqueraded as Henry VIII at a Brighton ball.

A number of these Tobies were produced, one of the potters thought to be **Ralph Wood**. They are 14", 15" and 16" high. The figure is always wearing a slashed doublet and a tricorn hat. In his right hand is a sword, his left arm forming the handle of the jug whilst his left hand holds a buckler, embossed with a crowned head and the initials 'GR', no doubt those of George IV. It was probably made to commemorate his coronation in 1820 and it is unlikely, in the light of the high quality of the jugs, that they were made later than this date.

There are variations of this jug, one in which the right hand is holding a wide-topped, stemmed glass instead of the usual mug of beer and a sword at his left side with a tall jug resting on the floor. Another version depicts Prince Hal with his left hand holding his sword scabbard. The bases are usually square, sometimes with an acanthus leaf motif or frogs on them, and the figure occasionally stands on rocky ground. **Value: £2500/$3750.**

There is a copy of this jug in silver lustre (*see under Lustre Tobies*).

Frank Falkner refers to this jug in his 1912 book *The Work of the Ralph Woods* as the 'Falstaff Jug' and is probably the best name (*see under Falstaff*).

One was sold at the Bute sale in July 1996, holding a sword in his right hand and a buckler in the left. Embossed with a lion's head, it was inscribed 'John of Gant' (sic). With a height of 15½" it sold for £5,520 including buyers premium even though it was badly damaged

Punch and Judy

Colour pictures on pages 72, 73 and 101.
These are the only Toby Jugs which have been made to sell as a pair, breaking with the usual practice of producing Tobies as single items (contrary to common belief). Both jugs are around 10" high. Punch usually wears striped clothes and a forward pointed conical hat (though this is often missing). He sits on a pile of books which are evidently volumes of *Punch*.

Judy is also sitting with her right hand in the pocket of her costume and her left hand holding a cane. She is sometimes dressed in a long white gown and apron, though she can also be found with a pale blue bodice and sleeves accompanying a red skirt. A third colour variation is an all yellow dress. Her shoes are usually black. The 'Punch and Judy' have an impressed registration mark no. 139844, the date

30 November, 1889. They were made by **William Machin** of Staffordshire, the date showing when they were first made. William Machin went out of business in 1911 and it is possible that the original moulds were acquired by **William Kent**, a mile and a half up the road, in Burslem. They were then produced there and still catalogued in 1962 with numbers: Punch 381 and Judy 382.

There is a second Punch Toby Jug, much less common than the above which was made in the middle of the nineteenth century possibly by one of the **Portobello** factories. It is painted in bright enamel colours — black, blue, maroon, cream, yellow and green and stands about 8" high.

James Dudson of Hanley shows in their sales ledger of 1842-44 that Punch and Judy Toby Jugs were being made by them and selling for 6 shillings (30p) a dozen, but sold as a pair. Presumably they were not marked, so it is not known what they looked like.

Puzzle Jug Toby
See under 'Yorkshire'.

The Reading Toby
Colour picture on page 99.
First listed by Captain Price, this Toby is very rare (only two being known) and of unknown origin. It is a Toby holding an open book in both hands and is beautifully modelled, standing 11" high. Probably made by the same potter who made 'The Bottle Toby', 'Wineskin Toby' and 'Rodney's Sailor' with bottle in left hand. **Value: £2500/$3750.**

There is another Toby reading, 5" high but in the form of a money box. In creamy yellow streaked in blue, in coloured glazes, made c1800. Apart from this one I own, I've never seen another. The reason they are so rare is because you have to break the figure to get the coins out, although they can be removed by inserting a knife into the slot. There are a number of Staffordshire figures made around this time showing people reading as illiteracy was rife and to show a person reading was a novelty.

Roman Nose Toby
See under 'Shield Toby'.

Sailor Astride Barrel
This is a diminutive Toby Jog. At first glance one would not think it was a jug at all. Only 6" high, showing a sailor sitting astride a barrel smoking a pipe held in his left hand, his right hand is resting on the barrel holding a mug of ale. The sailor has a blue coat with striped trousers, whilst the barrel is green. The Jug which has some restoration work, a complete replacement handle sold at the Bute sale in July 1967 for £2500 with buyers premium.

Shield Toby
Colour picture on front cover and page 75.
An Ordinary type of Toby, 9¾" or 10" high in coloured glazes, which has a boat shaped shield on his side which has inscribed on it 'It is all out, then fill him again' (sic). The misspelling of 'again' appears to be common to all these jugs and in the Midlands 'again' was often pronounced 'again'. The face of Toby may vary a little in that the nose may be 'snubbed' (as on the Ordinary Toby) or of the large Roman Nose type. Sometimes Toby is smoking a pipe. **Ralph Wood** may have been the sole potter and Lord Mackintosh was under the impression that there were only six in existence. Sold Christies, London, 1989 **£4500/$6750**. Twelve have now been recorded.

When this jug is minus the shield it is called 'The Roman Nose Toby'.

Ralph Wood, Shield Toby c1780.

Small Sailor/Large American Sailor
Colour picture on pages 74 and 75.
Sometimes called 'The Small Sailor' or 'American Sailor'. The former because it is smaller than 'The

Rodney Sailor', or the latter because 'Dollars' is often written on one or both sides of the sea chest he is sitting on. 'The Sailor' is not American though, because on the jug he is holding is written 'Success to our Wooden Walls', which refers to the British tall-sided battleships with their four rows of guns. When the inscription is present it is surrounded by a heart shape or a floral pattern, but is occasionally all white without any inscription.

The 'Small Sailor' sits on a sea chest and is dressed in blue, though sometimes his trousers are white, with blue stripes down them. His waist length jacket is fastened by two rows of white buttons and he wears white socks with black shoes and buckles. He also wears a black scarf and hat with a detachable crown (often missing). The sailor's hair is gathered at the back of the head into a tarred pig-tail or 'queue'. The large overflowing jug of ale marked 'Success to our Wooden Walls' is in his right hand, resting on his thigh, whilst his left hand rests on his left thigh, holding a clay pipe. The base depicts a green, grassy mound and running up the back, forming the handle, is the trunk of an oak-tree, the branches of which flow over the sea-chest and down the sides of it.

The Toby is in overglaze enamels and is 10" high, probably made in the first quarter of the nineteenth century. Captain Price is known to have had a copy with a 'W' impressed on the base, indicating to him that the maker was **Walton** (1818-25). A copy is in the Victoria and Albert Museum which was found during excavation on the Isle of Dogs in London's East End.

A further variation, larger than the above jug at 12" high is one in which a sailor sits astride the corner of a sea-chest. He seems to have a gum-boil in his mouth, it being slightly swollen on one side. This jug has been recorded with the Victory medallion embossed on the sea chest, as on 'The Trafalgar Toby'. Both of these small and large jugs are sometimes impressed with 'W', which could stand for 'Walton' or 'Enoch Wood'. **Sold 1990, £1800/$2700.** They are recorded with the figure wearing a red waistcoat with black neckscarf or yellow waistcoat and red neckscarf. The overglaze colours on these jugs do tend to flake rather badly.

One rare occasions one might find on the back of the sea chest a medallion of a sailing ship. On the large jug the sailor will be holding a clay pipe in his left hand which is supporting the jug on his knee, or it might be resting on top of the sea chest between his thighs.

The Rodney Sailor or The Planter

Colour picture on page 74 – See also under Kevin Francis
Not to be confused with the 'Rodney Jug', one sold at Christies, King Street in 1990 for **£3700/$5550.**

Two of these jugs have been found inscribed on the base 'Lord Hou', both Pratt-type, one can be seen in the Nottingham Castle Museum (*see under Lord Howe, page 33*).

These are the various names given to a very fine and rare Toby Jug 11½" high, of a sailor dressed in white trousers which are sometimes striped. The coat is blue, the waistcoat red, and he has a black neck scarf, black wide brimmed hat and black shoes with buckles on them. The number of stripes on each leg may vary from three on some jugs to fourteen on others. On one jug the trousers are checked and there is a small floral motif in the squares and on the waistcoat.

Another wears a blue coat, white trousers with blue stripes, a yellow waistcoat decorated with small blue rings and a white neck scarf with blue spots. The jug held in the left hand is painted in white and yellow with a floral spray. This Toby was made much later than the one referred to previously, about 1890, and the decoration on the clothes disguises his sailor profession somewhat.

'The Sailor' sits on a high backed chair, under which is a sea-chest with handles at each end. In the left hand and resting on one end of the chest is a large jug. In his right hand is a raised glass. The base of the jug is of a rocky

Left: Rodney Sailor. The only one recorded with arm outstretched. Note mark on knee where unknown object rested and was held in hand. Long Pipe has been added. Right: Rodney Sailor, late 18th century holding bottle.

mound, washed by lapping waves, and between his feet is a sea anchor.

The variations noted are: **Coats**: which are usually blue, sometimes with white lapels, or light brown with blue lapels. When the coat is olive green, pale manganese or slate blue, the lapels are usually yellow. **Hats**: the straw hats are like those worn c1800 with wide-awake brims, some were made with round dish type brims like bowler hats, or in the tricorn shape with sharp upturned brims and detachable hat crown.

Lord Mackintosh had one with a churchwarden clay pipe resting on the front of the sea-chest by the left leg. Ralph Wood is thought to be the originator of this Toby, sometimes with the mould number '65' on the base. Inscriptions noted on Ralph Wood Sailors are: 'W.B.C. Old Toby Grantham' and on the back in beautiful inscribed letters:

Left and right 'American Sailors', Pearlware c1820. Centre 'Rodney Sailor', Creamware c1790. Rare wearing tricorn hat.

> 'Hallo, Brother Briton
> Whoever thou may be
> Sit down on
> That chest of hard dollars by me,
> And drink a health,
> To all sealors (sic) bold.'

And on another Ralph Wood Sailor is:

> 'Dollars jolly Jack Tar
> Just come from far, drink round brave boys.'

Other potters made this Toby, though probably not later than c1820, the exception being a model thought to be produced by **William Kent** of Burslem around 1900. One of these had cracks painted on the underside of the base and around the legs, probably in an attempt to fake the original. There are blue and white Delft type sailors which are probably around 1900 or later and might not be English.

The Planter

It is not clearly perceptible as to how this name came about. When the model of 'The Sailor' holds a plug of tobacco in his left hand as well as the jug, the Toby is often called 'The Planter', although the sea anchor might still be down between his feet. However, it is argued by some that only when the anchor is omitted is it called 'The Planter', while others only when the figure is wearing a tricorn hat. All these jugs are rare but this latter jug is very rare, I've only seen one, which is in my possession.

The bow of the anchor is sometimes missing which seems to point that the shaft of the anchor was part of the moulded base and the bow a separate moulding.

There is a very rare Pratt-type sailor wearing a blue coat and yellow trousers. His right arm is outstretched as if he was supporting something on his knee, as on his right knee ¾" x ³/₁₆" of the glaze is missing exposing the unglazed earthenware. After going through Sotheby's, Bond Street, auction rooms twice unsuccessfully with an estimated reserve price of £2000-£2500/$3000-$3750, it finally went to Sotheby's at Chester where it sold for a little over **£1000/$1500.**

I finally purchased it in the Portobello Road, London, at 5 o'clock one April morning for **£1450/$2175** and will probably spend the rest of my life trying to find out what our 'Jolly Jack Tar' was holding on his knee, unless another turns up or I am informed. This I think is all part of the fun of being a collector.

The Trafalgar Toby

Colour picture on page 73.

This is a sailor which wears a blue coat, white trousers and a white waistcoat with blue horizontal stripes. He also wears a black wide-brimmed sailor's hat. 'Trafalgar' is engraved on the handles of the sea-chest which is situated under the chair. On the back of the chest, between the chair legs is a medallion of Nelson's flagship, Victory (all in enamel colours). It is suggested that this jug was made at the **Wood** factory c1815 and there are only seven known examples. The jug held in the left hand is smaller than usual.

The Rodney Sailor with Bottle

Colour pictures on pages 65.
Another very rare version of the 'Rodney Sailor' holds in his left hand a bottle in place of the jug and on his head wears a large tricorn hat in place of the usual sailor's wide awake hat. Also the face is different to the usual sailor with staring eyes. There are only seven of these jugs recorded. Six have a cupids bow front to the base and one a conventional rocky base, with rounded front. On four of these jugs, in place of sailors trousers the figure wears breeches with high boots halfway up his shins, and one figure sports a moustache and beard which are applied and not painted on. This jug sold at Sotheby's London in 1988 for **£9350/$14000**. It is thought that these jugs were made by the same potter who made the 'Reading', 'Wineskin', 'Bottle Between Legs' and 'Viscount Jarvis' jugs.

There is some doubt as to whether some of these jugs are as early as first thought, maybe nineteenth century and not eighteenth century. Captain Price refers to this sailor as a **later** representation of the Ralph Wood model.

Some of the above-mentioned Tobies have a large raised 'V' on the left side of the hat brim. The eyes are heavily lined in black and the potting is cruder, so these I believe to be later jugs, one can be seen in the Liverpool Museum, Merseyside. Myra Brown, Ceramics Curator, informs me that the collection of over fifty tobies were presented to the Museum by George Audley in 1926, so this Toby must have been made before this date, but when or by whom is as yet unknown to me.

One of the eighteenth century Jugs was sold at the Bute sale in July 1996. This figure was holding in his right hand an oval tazza of food. The Jug was 11½" high, restored and the sale price with buyer's premium was £3450.

Sailor with Tall Jug

A sailor Toby 12⅝" high in the form of a man sitting on a coiled rope and anchor. He is holding in his hands and resting on his left knee and shoulder a 6¼" high slender baluster vase shaped jug. The figure is missing his hat, so we don't know what it looked like, as there appears not to be another recorded. This jug was sold at Christie's South Kensington, London on 21 November 1996 for £2070 with buyer's premium.

Viscount Jarvis

Colour picture on page 66.
A further variant of the 'Rodney Sailor' with brown and orange coat. The sea-chest is not as wide, so he balances the jug held in his left hand on his knee. The Toby is only 8" high. Incised on the base is 'Visct Jarvis', only one of these jugs is recorded which was in R.K. Price's collection. See in his book Fig 143. **Value: over £2000/$3000.**

Hearty Good Fellow Sailor

Colour picture on page 71.
When the 'Hearty Good Fellow' wears trousers in place of breeches, which are white with blue stripes and the coat is blue, white waistcoat with blue horizontal stripes, he becomes a Standing Sailor. Rare.

The Shepherd

Colour picture on page 75.
An extraordinary Toby, although a common Pratt-type Ordinary with blue coat, made c1800. But, added are two sheep, one standing on the figure's right arm, the other standing between his legs and looking up to his face. Despite the hat being completely replaced, or at least repaired and repainted and a crack right down the face, it sold at Sotheby's London in October 1989 for **£4180/$6270,** but it is the only one recorded. Maybe it was made for a local shepherd who asked the potter to make him a Toby, but one would think that if this was so his name would be on the jug.

I have recently been informed that there are other copies of this jug in the United States. If this is so, they might well turn up yet at auction.

At the Bute sale in June 1996, an ordinary Toby in Pratt colours was sold, the same as the Shepherd, but this Toby figure was holding a monkey in uniform blowing a trumpet (this had been added to the original jug). I have examined both jugs, the Shepherd was seven years ago, at that time I was not suspicious, but I am now. I think maybe the sheep were also added. This jug was in very bad condition but sold for £1495 with buyer's premium.

The Snuff Taker

Colour picture on page 75.

Sometimes referred to as the 'Benjamin Franklin' Toby', owing to its said likeness to the eighteenth century American statesman, philosopher and inventor, 1706-90. He lived in England for eighteen years and he probably took snuff, as it was the fashion of the time.

The jug is in the form of a pot-bellied man taking a pinch of snuff from a box held in his left hand. It is the most common of all Toby Jug types and it can be found in **Rockingham** treacle glaze, brown saltglaze, overglaze enamel, plain white and silver lustre (the latter giving a pleasing effect when slightly worn off, exposing the brown glaze underneath leaving a ghostly, ethereal appearance). He is generally modelled quite poorly, although there are some attractive 4" versions to be found. Some variations have a spout rising out from under his pot-belly which transforms the 'Snuff Taker' into a teapot in the most startling manner (not to be used when your maiden aunt comes to tea!). **£100/$150+.**

Snuff Taker teapot c1850.

There are rare and very interesting stoneware versions of the 'Snuff Taker'. Two jugs are notable because of their similarities and their differences. One is about 7" high, holding a square snuff box upside down at arms length, the whole jug being coloured and slightly glazed. The figure is inscribed on the base, 'A.C. Pope 1829', which tells us that the 'Snuff Taker' has been in production since at least that date. The other stoneware 'Snuff Taker' holds the square snuff box in the more conventional manner and is slightly different in that it is much harsher and brighter than the other, almost a majolica. This jug is not signed, but was obviously made by the same potter.

There were a great many makers of this jug over the years and there are consequently a great number of different types. **William Kent** of Burslem was making the 'Snuff Taker' from c1900 up to 1962 (mould no. 390), and **Allerton and Son** had another long production run from c1859-1942. The Allerton 'Snuff Takers' usually have some lustre and gilt decoration on them, the figure wearing a blue coat.

Another maker was **Sharpe Brothers and Co.** who made a 'Snuff Taker' and a companion female standing figure in a long dress. This is in majolica-ware with a glaze running up the figure, varying from yellow to green. It is a poorly modelled jug, made c1880 (*see Lady Toper*).

Snuff Taker type with Jug c1840.

It is possible to find a 6" high Staffordshire enamel overglaze Toby in a blue mottled coat which is the same pot-bellied standing figure as the 'Snuff Taker'. In place of the snuff box in his left hand, he holds a large pot and in his right, a foaming jug of ale (*see under Standing Toby*).

All of these snuff taking Tobies and their kindred drinkers have a base which is adorned with a bacchus motif of vine leaves and bunches of grapes.

The 'Snuff Taker' is very common and because he came later than the Ordinary (from around 1830), it is difficult to find any that were made in the quality of the early period.

James Dudson of Hanley show in their sales ledger of 1842-44 that 'Snuff Taker' Toby Jugs were being made by them and selling for 4 shillings (20p) per dozen, but it is not known the size of these jugs.

Small 'Snuff Takers' around 6" high were made by **Sampson Smith**, and where marked (not always the case) in raised capital letters. *See also under 'Tumbler Toby', John Carrol.*

Value of all these jugs is under £150/$225.

The Soldier

Colour picture on page 76.

An Ordinary Toby which gets its name because he is wearing a long red coat with yellow buttons (for brass), yellow breeches, a black tricorn hat and black shoes, which all fit in with the clothing of an eighteenth century soldier. His white hose has a number of wavy blue stripes running down the leg.

These Tobies may look as though the faces have lost their crispness, possibly through the use of old worn moulds, but the glory of this Toby is the very fine 'sparrow beak' Pratt-type jug of foaming ale held on the knee. This is a typical jug style of the 1830s. £150/$225+.

Squat Toby

Colour picture on page 98.

Is the name which is given to the group of Toby Jugs where Toby is sitting on the ground with his legs up to his chest and crossed in front. One version of this was probably made around 1840 and produced entirely in copper or silver lustre. The earliest ones have a pink interior with a pink lustre wavy line around the inside at the top.

However, it is more common to find the jugs in enamel colours. These jugs were produced throughout the nineteenth century, and **William Kent** of Burslem still had them catalogued as late as 1962 (though these later ones are poorly painted and lacking in detail). All these Tobies are between 4" and 6" high.

Some have a rustic type handle on them which may either have a normal handle top or one which is forked. The ones with the forked handle are usually the better quality jugs and are much more interesting.

There is also another 'Squat Toby' in this group. It is a short, dumpy Toby made by **Copeland Late Spode** of Stoke. These are 6" high and very colourful, in bright enamels with patterned/floral coats. The mark on the base is a sailing boat with a laten triangular sail indicating that it was made c1900.

One of these Squat Tobies is marked 'Romney Pottery'.

Value: under £100/$150 for all these jugs

See also 'Loving Cup Toby' and Lustre Tobies.

The Squire

Colour picture on page 76

A fine **Ralph Wood** original of 'The Squire' can be seen in the Victoria and Albert Museum and another at the Stoke-on-Trent Museum. A most distinctive jug. It depicts a thin, gaunt gentleman with a beaky nose and long lank hair down to his shoulders. He is sitting on a corner chair wearing a long coat, knee breeches and hose, neck-scarf and buckled shoes. He clutches a jug of foaming ale to his belly with his right hand, whilst he holds a churchwarden clay pipe with his left. The base is an unusual shape, completely flat on the underside, height is 11" or 12". The exception seems to be the Ralph Wood which has a ⅜" recess.

Shape of
'The Squire'
base

It is said Ralph Wood senior originally modelled this jug and, if one compares it to a portrait of his father in Frank Falkner's book *The Wood Family of Burslem*, one can see a striking resemblance between the two. However, with the speculation about Ralph Wood senior's potting status and his work for Wedgwood, we may even suggest that the jug was originally modelled by Ralph Wood II in the likeness of his grandfather — but perhaps this is going too far.

The hat crown and pipe are invariably missing from the earlier models. The early 'Squire' holds the pipe in his left hand with index finger and thumb resting on top of the stem whilst the later nineteenth century 'Squire' holds his pipe by the thumb alone. On twentieth century models there is no hole at all, even under the thumb, in which to place a pipe. Some potters in this late period have attempted to make a hole for the hand to accommodate a pipe but have not bothered to pierce the hole through properly, thereby dispensing with the whole idea of a pipe. This is an indication of the creeping decadence of Staffordshire pottery over time. This jug has been much reproduced in the past 200 years, one of the potters being **William Kent** (of the Staffordshire pottery).

The eighteenth century 'Squire' was

Three Squires. Left: Wood & Sons c1975; Centre unknown, probably twentieth century and made from W. Kent moulds; Right William Kent c1900.

made in the translucent coloured glazes, whereas the nineteenth century versions had enamel cobalt blue coats or overglaze brown coats. These are the most common, but there are many variations. Sometimes underglaze mottled patterns are found which are quite attractive and they are a must for the avid collector who cannot afford the original. These jugs were still in the Kent catalogue (No. 380) in 1962, and the **Gladstone** pottery of Longton was still potting them in 1975. The Kent 'Squire' usually sells for around **£200/$300** whilst a Ralph Wood type sold in 1990 for **£5000/$7500**.

Four Squires. From left: unknown nineteenth century; probably Ralph Wood c1780; William Kent c1880; William Kent c1950.

The 'Squire' with the mottled horseshoe effect at one time was thought to have been made in the early nineteenth or even late eighteenth century. However, this appears to not be so, for no photographs appeared before around the 1970s of this jug, also as far as I know, the first time one came up in auction was in 1975. There is evidence that they were being made in Burslem in the 1960s. Sotheby's had one on view at the 1990 Fine Art and Antiques Fair at Olympia, London 'as a fake' (*see under Fakes*). The face and hands were too white for either **pearlware** or **creamware**. Probably made from William Kent moulds.

Although the 'Squire' is generally credited to **Ralph Wood**, there appears as yet, to be no real evidence.

Most 'Squires', both early and late, show the figure holding a pear shaped jug in his right hand, over or resting on his right knee. Occasionally on eighteenth century 'Squire's the small jug is bulbous in shape and is held between the knees. Also on these early jugs the base may be found to be recessed on the underside.

There is one 'Squire', found occasionally, 12" in height, when looking at the tricorn hat from the front, the left side protrudes ½" farther than on the right, and is more rounded. Inside the hat at forehead level is a rim for a hat crown to rest upon. The hands are very well modelled and a pipe is held between the first and second fingers of the left hand.

The Squire, probably R. Wood c1785. Note position of the small agate jug.

The jug shown at the far left in the bottom picture on page 76 is in a cream tin glaze with a pale green coat with the glaze running down the chair, blue waistcoat with mottled brown hat and shoes.

One other was sold at the auction rooms of C. B. Sheppard & Sons in April 1991 for **£235/$350**. This had a red coat, yellow breeches, blue-green waistcoat and was sitting on a pale blue chair between the legs of which are floral sprigs. The maker of these 'Squires' is unknown to me, but the floral decoration points to a continental manufacturer.

The only other Tobies I know with a rim inside the hat is the 11" high majolica Ordinary and a similar jug sold at Christies, King Street, London on 16th July, 1979. Both these very rare jugs had finely modelled hands. The date and manufacturer are unknown but possibly Portuguese.

The William Kent moulds are still owned by the family and loaned out to potters who are reproducing them. At this time Bairstow Manor Pottery are using them and they are putting the hole in the left hand to take the pipe.

See also under William Kent, Kevin Francis and Bairstow Manor Pottery.

The Step Toby

Colour picture on page 77.

It is not easy to state which are the first Toby Jugs made after the Dighton Print in 1761, it could be 'The Step Toby', or, as once called, 'The Twyford Toby'. As to who gave it this name it is hard to determine. One possibility is **Joshua Twyford**. It is said that he worked along with Astbury and Whieldon for the Elers brothers, John and David, during the early part of the eighteenth century. Other than this little is known of him, but he had a pot bank near Shelton Church.

But the name Twyford can be seen on ceramic wares in public lavatories, no doubt a descendant more 'flushed' with success than the early maker of our Toby Jug!

The 'Step Toby' is so called because of the recessed underside of the base, which is more shallow under the feet than under the rest of the jug so making a step. The base on the outside is thinner than on most other Tobies, only ½" high. The 'Rodney', 'Midshipmite' and 'Fiddler' jugs also have step bases.

The jugs are in creamware, usually the figures are smoking pipes held in the right hand, whilst the other holds a pear shaped jug, either empty, or may be full of foaming ale. The feet are hollow.

But there are variations, such as the one in the author's collection where the right hand is supporting the small jug on the knee and holding his pipe, the stem of which rests along the arm. The small jug is hollow right through. This jug is complete with its original hat crown. Rarely one may be found with the hand holding the pipe lower down so that the pipe stem is held away from the mouth. Occasionally a dog may be found lying between his feet or by his right foot. One has appeared with a beard and another with boots halfway up his shins. Despite being early, it is surprising the frequency with which they appear in the specialist sales of English pottery. **Sold Christies, 1989. £850/$1275.**

The Standing Man Toby

There are a number of types of this jug, four of which we concentrate on here. This jug is in the form of a man standing on a round stippled base, the whole in varying polychrome colours, about 10" high. The jug is reminiscent of Portobelloware, standing four-square holding a jug in his left hand and a pipe in his right, being moulded into the body.

One type of Standing Toby is 6¼" high holding a jug in both hands. This little jug was probably made at Portobello c1830 in underglaze enamels: blue, black, green and maroon. Another stands 6" high, in Staffordshire enamel overglaze, has a mottled blue coat, which is the same pot-bellied standing figure as the 'Snuff Taker' who holds the more traditional large jug in his right hand and a mug of foaming ale in his left. A similar of 'Snuff Taker' origin is a

Three Standing Tobies: Left and right: Portobello c1840 and centre a c1980 reproduction.

figure in enamel colours clutching a foaming jug of ale to his chest in both hands. He has a smiling face with a large upturned nose and stands 9¼" high. There is another 10¾" high with small jug moulded into body.

These standing Tobies of the snuff taker type have a base in keeping with the Ordinary 'Snuff Taker' with bacchus motifs of vine leaves and bunches of grapes around them. *See also: 'Black Man', 'The Barrister', 'The Hearty Good Fellow',' Nelson', 'The Snuff Taker' and Rockingham.*

This Toby also appears in Rockingham Brown Treacle Glaze, majolica, in a pale all over green glaze, and as a 'Black Man', c1840.

There are recent reproduction models of this Toby which are quite good, but they are let down a little by poor painting on the face and heavy, exaggerated crackle. The reproduction model is a little smaller at 9½" high. On the underside of one of these earlier jugs is marked 'T. Burnell. London'.

The Thin Boy

Colour picture on page 77.

The name for this jug was first suggested by Eric Hudes in the 1950s and is possibly made by the same potter who made 'The Thin Man', but instead of holding a glass or a pipe in the right hand the figure is steadying a jug on his knee. The face has fat boyish cheeks and the right hand side of the mouth is turned up into a leer. This is a very rare Toby, even rarer than 'The Thin Man'. Two sold at Sotheby's London, 1985, **£2500/$3750** (one was badly damaged).

The Thin Man

Colour picture on pages 77 and 116.

An aristocrat of the Tobies. As is implied by his name, he is a slender man, only 3" wide and 9" tall. He has a grinning cadaverous face and his hair has a curly fringe. He is wearing a tricorn hat, short coat, breeches, hose and buckled shoes. He is sitting on a Chinese Chippendale type chair and in his left hand is a brown jug, sometimes full, but more often than not empty. He usually smokes a clay pipe which is held to his mouth by his right hand. A variation of this is a figure with a glass instead of the pipe. There is one with a pipe down by right leg.

This is an eighteenth century jug c1770, in beautiful running coloured glazes. The modelling is superb. There is no degree of certainty as to who made 'The Thin Man', Ralph Wood, Whieldon and Leeds all having been suggested, but as there is no evidence that Whieldon ever made any Toby Jugs, it is unlikely to be he, but it is a desirable jug by any standards (see also under Kevin Francis). Sold, Christies, London 1989, £4200/$6300.

Thin Man with glass.

The Tipsy Man

Colour picture on page 77.

Lord Mackintosh considered that this jug was unique, the rarest in his collection. It is slightly larger than the Ordinary Toby at just under 11" high. The small jug is larger than usual and overflowing with ale. The coat is beautiful soft blue-grey and on his head is a tricorn hat with a detachable crown which can be used as a cup. The chair which Toby sits on is unusual in that it leaves Toby's feet free-standing rather than on a plinth. The jug was sold at Sotheby's on 2 May, 1967 for **£480/$720**.

However, this is not a unique Toby, as Lord Mackintosh thought. A similar model is illustrated in Bernard Hughes' book, *English and Scottish Earthenware*, but it is not the same jug since it is a Portobello Toby, painted in polychrome colours beneath the glaze, and obviously made in the nineteenth century. I feel however that this observation is more than a little suspect and it is indeed a coloured glazed jug of the eighteenth century. For this self same jug was sold by Sotheby's at a house sale in East Lothian, Scotland on 22 May, 1990 for **£16500/$24750**, which is believed to be the highest price paid for a Toby Jug to date, outside the 'Midshipmite' group. The detachable hat crown was missing. One other 'Tipsy Man' recorded, was sold at Hove in Sussex c1986 for **£5200/$7800**, but this had quite a lot of damage. Sotheby's, London sold one on 14 April, 1992, complete with hat crown. This jug was in creamware painted in enamel colours, and printed on the large jug held in the left hand is 'strong ale', hat chip, restored hat crown and left foot. The hammer price with VAT and premium was **£9000/$13500**.

One sold at Sotheby's, London on 13 June 1995 for £6500. This Jug was 10¼" high (rim chips and one leg restored).

At the Bute Collection sale at Christies King Street, London on 8 July 1996, one was sold for £4025 with buyers premium. Part of his hat brim was missing, also the base. This Jug has now been nicely restored.

This makes six 'Tipsy Men' recorded to date.

Tithe Pig & Parson Jug

Colour picture on pages 77 and 78.

An extremely rare jug. It stands 11¾" high and represents the 'Parson of the Tithe Pig' Group, possibly made first by **Ralph Wood** and by various other potters including **Lakin and Poole** of Burslem in 1791, showing a peasant farmer's wife offering her baby in payment of tithe instead of the pig held by her husband. This Toby depicts the Parson standing, holding a glass in his left hand, almost at arms length. Inscribed on the yellow square pillar by his side are the words 'I will have no child tho the pig'.

The figure has a detachable crown to the hat which can be used as a drinking cup, but on some copies the crown is fixed which makes it impossible to use as a jug, although it still retains its handle.

This jug and tithe pig figures in general were no doubt inspired by the following lines written in the eighteenth century:

> In a country village lives a Vicar
> Fond as all are of tythes and liquor
> To mirth his ears are seldom shut
> He'll crack a joke and laugh at smut.
> But when his tythes he gathers in

True Parson then, no coin no grin
On fish on flesh on birds and beast
Alike lays hold the churlish priest
Hal's wife and sow as gossips tell
Both at a time in pieces fell
The Parson comes the pig he claims
And the good wife with taunts inflames
But she quite arch bow'd low and smiled
Kept back the pig, held out the child.
The Priest look'd gruff the wife looked big
'Zounds Sir' quoth she, 'No child no pig.'

There is a similar jug, equally rare, and now in Kansas City, Missouri, USA. This differs from the above mentioned jug in many ways, chief of which is that the Parson is not holding his arm outstretched and a large pig is standing by his right leg. In his arms he is cradling a baby. The jug is glaze stained with grey and splashes of orange. It is 10½" high and made c1770. There is another like the last jug mentioned but minus the large pig.

I know of seven of these Tobies.

Town Crier

This jug is in the form of a standing man, holding a parchment in his left hand from which he is reading a proclamation. His right arm stretches up and out and he holds a gilt bell in his hand. The coat may be brown, blue or green and the waistcoat is usually pink or yellow.

These Tobies come in four sizes, 1½", 4", 7½" and 8¾". Possibly made in the twentieth century this Toby is likely to have been manufactured in Germany or France, but there is a lot of confusion about it when it comes up for auction in Britain. These jugs are usually porcelain, **Sampson** of Paris often suggested as the maker. They are heavy, with a gold anchor mark under the handle. The Toby does not look incongruous in a collection of British Toby Jugs and, being unusual, makes it quite collectable. **£75/$112+.**

One other copy of this gives further scope for consideration because it is made of pottery, is 9½" high and quite lightweight compared to the porcelain ones. It has the gold anchor mark under the handle, indicating that it was made by the same potter as the above. The base has a 1⅜" deep recess to accommodate a musical box movement.

Henry Sandon informs me that the Jugs with the gold anchor were made at 'Sitsendorf', Germany and not Sampson of Paris.

Trafalgar Toby

See under 'The Sailor'.

Tumbler Toby

Colour picture on page 76.
A brown salt-glazed stoneware jug of the Ordinary type. Toby holds a tumbler in his right hand, similar in relative size to the pint glass we have today. His left hand rests on the left knee, the Toby being 8" in height with the word 'Fulham' inscribed in free hand on the base.

Fulham marks are inscribed 'Fulham, C. J. C. Bailey 1864-1889' sometimes with the monogram said to be that of John Carrol. However, James R. Cruickshank also worked at Fulham and used the same monogram. He later moved to Doultons at Lambeth.

In the Victoria and Albert Museum can be seen one of these Tobies marked 'J. C. FULHAM'.

Another seen which is a 'Snuff Taker' has the letter 'R' impressed. This has a silver hat rim around the top of the hat hallmarked at Birmingham 1885 and yet another 'Snuff Taker' is holding his open snuffbox upside down. This Toby is highly glazed and incised 'Fulham'.

Some of these jugs are either found all-over glazed, unglazed, partly glazed, leaving the face, hands, breeches and tumbler unglazed. They all have a plain 4¾" 'C' scroll handle.

The Toby holding a tumbler seems to be peculiar to the Fulham Pottery. The pot-bank became the **Fulham** Pottery and Chevin Filter Co Ltd c1889-1920. **£150/$225+.**

Unfrocked Parson

See under 'Drunken Parson'.

The Village Idiot

Colour picture on page 78.

This is basically an Ordinary Toby made in the late eighteenth century with coloured glazes which are typical of those by **Ralph Wood**, though it is not thought to be by him.

The jug has been so called because of the particularly bewildered look on the toper's face. The potter is unknown. Captain R.K. Price had one of these jugs with 'John Barlow' inscribed on front of base under the feet. One sold Sotheby's 1988 **£1760/$2640.**

The Welshman

Colour picture on page 78.

Another very rare Toby Jug, said to represent Sir Watkins Wynn, the head of a well known North Welsh Border family. He is depicted as a sitting man with a tricorn hat, his head turned slightly to the side. A goat lies behind his striped stocking clad legs. It is worth noting that the goat is still the Regimental Mascot of the Welsh Guards.

The chair on which he sits has a sword and shield on the back. The Welshman holds a foaming jug of ale in his left hand and balances it on his knee in the conventional manner. The jug in hand is decorated with floral sprigs and is moulded into body of main jug, which is very uncharacteristic of an eighteenth century Toby. It has been claimed that this Toby was made by **Ralph Wood**, but it has not the characteristics of a typical Wood-type. Two were sold at the Christie's Bute Collection sale in June 1996 for £9775 and £4370 with buyer's premium.

Only six have been recorded.

George Whitfield Toby (Nightwatchman)

Whoever bestowed the name 'The Night-watchman' on this jug got it all wrong. The clothes and wig are too refined to have been worn by a nightwatchman. It is far more likely to be the figure of George Whitfield, a famous Methodist preacher (1714-70) who was a friend of John Wesley. The reason for this possibly is that in Joseph Reed's play *The Register Office*, produced in 1761, Whitfield is introduced as 'Mr Watchlight'. The lantern was symbolic of his lifelong fight to proclaim The Light of the World, and in fact Whitfield was known for his sermons which were often made at night, under the light of a lamp. This could have been the reason for his confusion with a nightwatchman. Another tell-tale sign which points to the fact that it is Whitfield, is that he is known to have a squint due to an attack of measles when a boy, and this squint is reproduced in his face (though not always apparent in later reproductions).

Of all the Toby Jugs made, this is surely the most unusual. Instead of the more conventional figure standing or sitting, with the tricorn hat acting as a spout, this figure sits on a chair holding a lantern in his right hand which is down between his feet, his left hand clutching a broad brimmed hat to his chest. His head carries a full bottomed wig known as a 'physical' c1780 – the same type as that worn by 'The Drunken Parson'. The back of the chair acts as the jug's spout and the handle is formed by the right hand holding the lantern. The figure is usually wearing a long coat which flows over the plinth which is usually marbled, splashed with a stippled pattern, or it may be plain with a red-brown line around it. The figure is in both over and underglaze colours and stands 9½" high.

There is one very unusual copy of this jug in Liverpool Museum, in as much that the right arm is raised and in the hand is held what appears to be an onion shaped bottle. Unfortunately the bulbous part of the bottle is broken off, so it is not certain if it is a bottle, but a bottle is not in keeping with George Whitfield, who is not known as an imbiber.

A smaller version of this jug stands 8" high. It differs in that the lantern is resting on the figure's left knee instead of the floor between his legs. There are two different models of the jug, the earliest and rarest being a figure with the smaller lantern, being held by both hands at the base. The slightly later jug has a larger lantern which is held by the figure halfway up its side with the left hand, the right hand resting on top (*see picture page 65*).

The white base has flat sides and back with a rounded front like 'The Drunken Parson'. Made by

Three different types of George Whitfield Tobies. The one on the right is probably the earliest by Enoch Wood c1830.

51

Enoch Wood, who also made very fine pottery busts of both George Whitfield and John Wesley.

The larger figure continued to be reproduced right through the nineteenth and twentieth centuries up to 1960 by **William Kent**. Rare mark: **Enoch Wood** (c1790-1800). **£150/$225+.**

See also under Lustre Tobies.

Wineskin Toby

Colour picture on page 78.

An Ordinary type Toby, 11" high, but instead of having the usual jug on the knee, Toby holds a wineskin over a brazier which is situated in between his knees. It is a great rarity by an unknown potter, and it is not known when this was made. Only two have been recorded and were probably made by the same potter that made 'The Bottle Toby', 'Reading Toby' and 'Rodney Sailor' holding bottle. **Value: £2000/$3000**

Yorkshire Toby c1800-20

Colour picture on page 69.

is a believed provenance name given to a whole range of Ordinary Tobies, most of which have very unusual variations. This group of jugs vary greatly in quality, from Pearlware to Stoneware, some of the latter are quite crude. One assumes they were all made at the same factory, but it is not known for sure. The most commonly known of these Yorkshire Tobies is a very brightly coloured Pratt-type enamel underglaze, about 10" high. Many of these have a blue frock coat, yellow breeches and white tricorn hat, which is scalloped in black around the edges of the brim, though it is the sponging of underglaze colours on the base which is more typical of the 'Yorkshire' type. The hat brim is itself sometimes scalloped as well as the painting on the brim. The detail is more pronounced on some Yorkshire jugs than on others. These Yorkshire Tobies sometimes have the feature of the Toby holding another small Toby, held in the left hand and resting on the left knee. In his right hand, Toby holds a raised six-sided glass. He sometimes will also have a black and white spaniel dog between his feet. A long serpentine clay pipe rests on the side of Toby's chest, stretching from his shoulder to his pot belly. The back of the jug has a pale pastel green panel on which is fixed the white handle, which is a very handsome affair. The Yorkshire Toby handle is often in the form of a ship's figurehead, or a funeral tomb type figure with arms crossed across the chest.

The eyebrows are usually a series of black dots, Toby sporting a tiny black fringe whether the hair on his head is black or brown. The hat and the whole of the inside of the brim has a stippled pattern in blue, green and yellow. This stippling is also on the detachable crown of the hat and around the base of the jug.

On many of the jugs there is a crown impression on the base similar to that shown right. What might be of significance is that it is a Queen's crown as opposed to a King's crown, which would make these jugs later than 1837, when Queen Victoria came to the throne. But in all probability it was just a stylised crown with no bearing to the monarch at the time.

At one time Sotheby and Co were referring to this jug as a 'Wilson Toby' because an impressed crown device like his was used by **Isaac Wilson and Co** 1852-87, but this was at least fifty years too late for these jugs. As yet no one seems to know which pottery used the impressed crown device and used the stippled pattern in blue, green and yellow. At one time they were referred to in auction catalogues as being made in the Don pottery; the Mexborough pottery, the Middlesborough and the Swillington Bridge pottery have also been suggested. It seems inconceivable that no one seems to know, as the output of this unknown pottery was prolific in the production of Toby Jugs, cow creamers, watch stands, equestrian figures and others, but they are all referred to as 'Yorkshire'. Later imitations are common, with some of the same characteristics: the six-sided glass is in the right hand and a figurehead handle and a faintly moulded pipe on the body, but without the scalloped hat, small Toby Jug on knee or dog between feet. Other characteristics of the Yorkshire jugs are, the head of the figure is inclined slightly to his left and the neckscarf is tucked into the waistcoat and does not hang outside, such as on most other Tobies. Also the back hat brim is higher than the sides, but this is not so on all jugs. Some other variations: jug is all over a very dull putty colour, complete with Toby Jug on knee, dog between feet, curly pipe, figure head handle and marked with impressed crown on base, 10" high. One very unusual Yorkshire Toby complete with figure head handle holding glass and jug in the usual manner, but all over silver lustre, 9½" high. Value: **£500/$750**

Bottle and Goblet Toby

Colour picture on page 70.

In place of the usual Toby, with the pot in the left hand balanced on the left knee, a goblet 2¼" high is held in the left hand and a bottle in the right. These Tobies are 10" high in underglaze bright enamel colours. It is likely to have a ½" recessed base and has the same characteristics of the Yorkshire Toby, the same facial details and head inclined slightly to the left, the waistcoat opening at the top and the ten buttons down the length of the coat. The handle of the jug is also in the same large proportions as the Yorkshire Toby, but it is not in a human form.

It is evident that these jugs were made in Yorkshire around 1800-20. This Toby can be found with the bottle resting either on the right knee or the left, though still held in the right hand. One sold at Christies in 1980 for **£320/$480**.

There is also said to be a Toby of this form in brown salt glaze stoneware.

Bottle and Pipe Toby
Colour picture on page 69.
Very similar to the above mentioned Toby and was probably made by the same pottery in Yorkshire c1800. The goblet has been replaced by a 3¼" pipe, the bowl of it resting on the left knee. **£500/$750+.**

Pipe and Large Jug Toby
Colour picture on page 69.
A rare jug similar to the two jugs above, but differing in as much as the toper holds in his left fist a 4½" pipe, in his right a large 2" high jug, resting on the pipe bowl, which is at the side of his left leg. The jug is a dull putty colour stoneware, splashed over with dark brown. **£500/$750+.**

Puzzle Jug Toby
Colour picture on page 74.
A very rare Toby with spouts or tubes in three corners of Toby's tricorn hat. Working on the same principle as

Two Yorkshires. Left: ordinary; right unusual c1800. All over putty colour showing dog, pipe, Toby Jug and cup.

Two Yorkshire Tobies, c1800. Left showing unusual pipe and jug. Right: note the red face, pipe and Toby Jug.

the traditional puzzle jug made in Medieval times, the drinker must block off two of the tubes and the hole at the inside of the handle, the liquid being sucked up through the third tube. If the wrong tube is sucked, the liquid flows out onto the imbiber through the side of the jug, which is pierced. The jug was made in Yorkshire and impressed with a crown mark. Toby holds a Toby Jug on the left knee and the handle is of the figure head type. Sold at Christies, 1980 £750/$1125.

A more common Yorkshire Toby around 8" high is of a standing man holding a bottle in his left hand and a glass in his right. This also has a figure head and coloured stippling around inside of hat and on base. There are many small Tobies 3" and 5" high modelled on this jug, only those with the coloured stippling one would refer to as being 'Yorkshire'.

There is a Yorkshire Toby Ordinary type holding a small child on one knee and a Toby Jug on the other. This jug is impressed with the Crown mark £1000/$1500+.

Electioneering Toby
Inscribed on small jug.

> A bumper
> Milton
> For Ever

In Pratt colours, 9¾" high, c1807. Lord Milton was the son of Earl Fitzwilliam and was one of the candidates for the Yorkshire election of 1807. This Jug was sold at the Bute sale, July 1996, with restoration and handle restuck, sold for £1035 with buyers premium.

CHAPTER SEVEN

Rodney, Fiddler and Midshipmite Group

Some collectors consider these not to be Toby Jugs at all, mainly because they deviate so much from the standard Ordinary type. The very primitive modelling which has gone into them indicates that they could be very early and the name of Astbury has been linked with these Tobies, which would certainly date them before his death in 1743. Such an association would put them among the first of the British Tobies to be made, but they could also have been made at a later date by an unknown potter. They are called 'Astbury' or 'Astbury-type' because they are thought to resemble his figures which are primitively modelled with black staring eyes, but this resemblance is very slight indeed, and the connection is somewhat tenuous.

The Tobies in this group are mainly of men playing violins and viola de gambas. In the case of the 'Midshipmites' they hold a sword drawn from a scabbard and have a glass in the left hand. Variations of this group include an ironing Toby or 'The Tailor' as he is popularly known and 'The Farrier' (a blacksmith who shoes horses), wearing an apron and holding a pair of pincers. A Toby which has a glass in one hand and a jug in the other is most reminiscent of the Ordinary Toby, but it is very easy to see that it could not have been inspired by the Dighton mezzotint.

Actually it is the 'Rodney Jug' that really dates this group of Tobies. George Brydges Rodney (1719-92), and Admiral Samuel Hood defeated the French under the command of Admiral De Grasse, off Domenica in April 1782. The result of this success brought about the peace of Versailles in 1783 and Admiral Rodney was made Lord Rodney in May 1782. So, the mask mugs with the inscription around the head band 'Success to Lord Rodney' could not have been made before this date.

The 11¾" high Toby Jugs bear a striking facial resemblance to these mugs. For this reason they are known as 'Rodney Jugs', the only exception being the one with a beard. In all other respects, apart from the face, which is not a Rodney type face, it is a Rodney Jug — the height, the base, the position of the feet, the body and arms, even to the scalloped pattern around the hat. Apart from the faces all the other Tobies in this group, 'The Small Fiddlers', 'The Viola Da Gamba', 'Sportsman', 'The Small Tailor', 'The Midshipmites' (or Soldiers), 'The Farrier' and "the Drummer' appear in the same style of modelling and they all had stepped bases.

As collectable and costly as this group of jugs are, they do all have a naivety more in keeping with the pottery of John Astbury and Thomas Whieldon than the later work of Ralph and John Wood, or their contemporaries of around 1785. What should settle the matter once and for all is the two following factors, firstly, that a Fiddler jug was sold at Sothebys in London on the 16 October 1967, inscribed on the underside: *Ruchard Darby Sep. 21. 1787.* In view of this I think it proves beyond doubt that the Fiddler jugs were all made around this date and not before. To add confusion, after checking the local Parish registers, neither 'Darby' or 'Derby' occurs as a surname in the eighteenth century. Secondly, at the Lord Mackintosh sale of his Toby Jugs at Sotheby's in London on 2 May, 1967, a Rodney jug was sold and according to the catalogue incised on the base in a cursive script was: *J. Marsh Jolley.* This meant nothing to me until 22 years later when, on 29 November, 1989, another Rodney jug was sold at Phillips in London, with the inscription on the base in a cursive script: *J. Marsh Folley.* Then the penny dropped, had Sotheby's misread the 'F' for a 'J'? A thing easily done in a cursive script with the inconsistent spelling of the day. But, the two 'Ls' were still there. Was it a misspelling for the name Foley? On checking, I found there was a Jacob Marsh whose pottery was shown on a map of Burslem dated 1800, and probably well established in the 1790s, but he moved to Lane Delph (close to Foley) in 1806 and the rate books show him to be working there until 1832 as Jacob Marsh of Golden Hill House (Foley) (*see picture page 65*).

This surely means that these two Rodney jugs were made after 1806 and probably all the other Rodney jugs as well. One may ask why the other Rodney and Fiddler jugs are not marked as well, I can only say for the same reason some R. Wood jugs are and others which are identical are not.

The rarity of these jugs, as well as their fetching naivety, makes them command a higher price than any other Toby Jug, whatever the quality. The Rodney jugs are particularly rare, with only 12 known to exist and, at 11¾", they are much bigger than the standard jug.

The 'Fiddler' jug has the distinction of being the most highly priced Toby jug to date. At Phillips Auction Room in London on 7 September, 1988 a 'Fiddler' sold for **£19000/$28500** (*see picture on page 65*). However, this figure was surpassed on the 18 October, 1988 at Sothebys, London, when another 'Fiddler' was sold for **£26000/$39000** (*see page 57*), the purchaser on both occasions was European Antiques (David Newbon) of New York. This same jug which belonged to Lord Mackintosh was sold in the same rooms on 2 May, 1967 (lot 54) when it was purchased by D.M.& P. Manheim for **£500/$750.**

It is interesting also to note that the 'Fiddler' jug has twice been reproduced this century. Six were made by Frank Stoner, a collector and antiques dealer before the first world war. One, in the possession of Mr Geoffrey Godden of Worthing (now in the author's collection), was made in the likeness of fellow collector F.S. Hooker. The following is a a letter sent to Mr Godden in 1963:

This toby was made as the result of dining with the late Mr F.S. Hooker, who had the most comprehensive collection of Toby Jugs ever assembled. After dinner he asked me, as he had done many times before, "When are you going to find me a 'Fiddler Toby?'" These are extremely rare and he did not have one in his collection. On my way home it occured to me that it would be interesting to make a fiddler toby for him, especially as he so resembled a toby himself. I lost no time in getting wax and modelling the jug. I then had moulds made and the jug was fired and decorated under my supervision.

When it was finished I took it home and placed it in the cabinet with my other pieces, and invited Mr. Hooker to the house. As usual, as soon as he entered the drawing room, he walked straight over to look at my collection of Staffordshire pottery, and immediately he spotted the Fiddler Toby, exclaiming, "Stoner, where did you get it — what a beauty." He then noticed the initials on the jug and enquired if I had any idea what they stood for. I told him that most probably they were the initials of the man for whom the Toby was made. By then I thought it was time to let him handle it, and he eventually turned it up and saw Frank Stoner incised on the base. I then presented it to him and explained how I had come to make it.

The sequel to it was that the following day he came rushing into my gallery in King Street to say that he had not been able to get home quick enough to show his wife, exclaiming "I've got my Fiddler at last!" Upon looking at it Mrs Hooker immediately cried, "Why, Stacy it is you!" It was in truth a portrait of him.

Only six were made. It would be interesting to know where the other five are now, including the original with the initials F.S.H. The jug stands 7" high (*see picture on page 100*). Very valuable. It has been said that the other five were made in the likeness of other well known collectors and the one shown is thought to be Lord Mackintosh.

The other reproduction was made by Beswick modelled by Mr Gredington in 1948. A nice little jug, a faithful copy of the original, but more sophisticated and of course in enamel colours where as the originals were all in coloured glazes. The jug is smaller than all the rest standing only 5¼" high compared to approx. 6½" of the originals.

The whereabouts of the 12 known Rodney jugs is not always easy to keep track of. The following is the last recorded whereabouts of the 'Rodney' and 'Midshipmite' jugs ('Farrier', 'Fiddler', 'Soldier', 'Tailor', 'Sportsman', 'Viola Da Gamba Player' and 'Drummer').

Rodney Jug

1. Captain R. K. Price collection – Soldier. Holding jug in right hand on knee, glass in left. Sword scabbard empty. 11¾".

2. Capt R. K. Price collection – Tailor. Ironing. Jug down by left leg. 11¾"

3. Stoke-on-Trent Museum – Descended from the Wood family in the Elizabeth Marianne Wood collection. Holding jug in left hand on knee. Pipe down by right leg. Glass held up in right hand. Brown streaky glaze running down forehead.

4. Willit Collection. Brighton Museum – Glass held in left hand. Jug on right knee.

5. Shown in *Early English Figure Pottery* by Sir Harold Mackintosh, 1938 – Farrier. Holding glass in left hand. Holding large jug in right on knee. Complete with hat crown.

6. Shown in *The Connoisseur* October 1906 by Gill & Reigate, 73-85 Oxford Street, London – Holding large jug on right knee, nothing in left. Man has vertical dashes for eyebrows and is sporting a beard (this is not a Rodney face).

7. Lord Mackintosh sale Sotheby's May 1967 from F.S. Berry collection – Fiddler. Holding fiddle in left hand, resting on knee. Glass in right hand. Jug down by left leg. 11¾" Inscribed 'Make the fiddler drink for why, with fiddling he is dry'. Bought by Manheim, £680/$1020.

8. Lord Mackintosh sale Sotheby's May 1967 from Stacey Hooker collection – Soldier, drawing sword from scabbard with his right hand.

Rodney Jug (11¾").

Holding funnel shaped glass in his left. Jug between feet. Complete with hat crown. 11½" inscribed: J. Marsh Jolley. Bought by Manheim, **£1050/$1575.**

9. Sold Sothebys 21st November 1953 – Sportsman. Sitting figure holding gun in his left hand, top of the barrel is missing, right hand holding jug on right knee, dog sitting between feet, pipe down by right leg. Handle of jug has brown acanthus and trellis decoration enriched with a blue florette. 11½" high.

10. Sold Phillips London 29 November, 1989 – Soldier. Sitting drawing sword (missing) with right hand on scabbard, left hand jug by right leg, glass down by left. Inscribed under base: J. Marsh, Folley. The head of this figure is missing and has been replaced with one made of bell metal. (This jug has since been beautifully restored, *see picture below and on page 65.*

11. Sold Fowler sale, Sotheby's Lot 77 29 October, 1961 –Holding a jug in right hand, and wine glass in left. Between his feet a spotted dog and a pipe by his right leg. 11". Bought by Cyril Andrade **£320/$480.** In Capt Price's book written in 1922 he states that he only knew of six of these jugs.

12. Sold Bute Collection Auction, Christie's King Street, July 1996 – Drawing sword from scabbard, part of which is missing, also pommel of sword. Height 11½", sold for £10,350 with buyers premium.

Fiddler (Small Size)

1. Captain R.K. Price collection –Playing fiddle, bow missing, jug down by right leg. 7½".

2. Captain R.K. Price collection from the Dr Sidebotham collection – Playing fiddle, large jug by right leg. 6½".

3. Stoke on Trent Museum – Playing fiddle, large jug by right leg.

4. Illustrated in *The Connoisseur* 1934. Article by Lord Mackintosh 'The Fun of Toby Jugs' – Playing fiddle. Approx. 6½"

5. Lord Mackintosh sale Sothebys May 1967 from F.S. Berry collection – A Rodney Jug. Holding fiddle in left hand on knee, glass in right hand, jug down by right leg. Inscribed: 'Make the fiddler drink for why, with fiddling he is dry'. Bought by Manhein, **£680/$1020.**

6. Sold Sothebys 1980 London – Playing Fiddle, legs crossed. 6¼". **£3500/$5250**

7. Sold Phillips London September 1988 – Playing fiddle. 7". **£19000/$28500.**

8. Sold Sotheby's London 18 October, 1988 – Playing fiddle complete with hat crown, large jug by left knee. 7". From the Mackintosh collection which sold in 1967 for £500/$750 – **£26000/$39000.**

9. Sold Sotheby's 16 October 1967 – Playing violin (bow and fiddle missing). 7¼". Underside of base is inscribed: 'Ruchard Darby Sep. 21. 1787'. Bought by C. Andrade. **£360/$540.**

10. Sold Bute Collection Auction, Christies, July 1996 – Playing fiddle, neck of which is missing, also bow and handle at back of Jug. Large Jug down by right leg. Sold for **£5750** with buyer's premium.

11. Brighton Museum – With Jug down by right leg.

From left: Tailor, second and fourth Fiddlers; third from left, Beswick Fiddler.

Fiddler 6⅞". Sold Sothebys in 1988 for £26000, the most expensive Toby Jug to date.

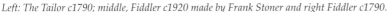

Left: The Tailor c1790; middle, Fiddler c1920 made by Frank Stoner and right Fiddler c1790.

Fiddler Jug 6¼". Sold Phillips, London in 1988 for £19000.

The Midshipman or Soldier (Large)

1. Captain R.K. Price collection – Rodney Jug. Holding jug in right hand and glass in left. Sword scabbard empty. 11¾".

2. Lord Mackintosh collection sold Sotheby's May 1967 – Rodney Jug. Complete with hat crown, holding glass in left hand, drawing sword from scabbard. 11½". Incised on base: 'J. Marsh Jolley'. Bought by Manheim for **£1050/$1575** from Stacey Hooker collection.

3. Lord Mackintosh collection sold Sotheby's May 1967 – Holding glass in left hand, sword in right. Sitting on chest. 7¾". Bought by Spink for £750/$1125.

4. Shown in article by Lord Mackintosh 'The Fun of Toby Jugs', *The Connoisseur* **1934** – Holding sword in right hand, glass in left, striped pants. Sitting on chest. Approx 6½".

5. Stoner and Evens, 3 King St, St James, London – Advert in *The Connoisseur* March 1912, holding glass in left hand, sword in right.

6. C. Andrade, 24 Ryder St, St James, London – Advert in *The Connoisseur* March 1914. Holding glass in left hand and large jug in right on knee.

7. C. Andrade, 8 Duke St, St James, London – Advert in *The Connoisseur* February 1920. Holding glass up to mouth in left hand and large jug in right. 6½".

8. Nelson-Atkins Museum, Kansas City, Mo, USA – Holding large jug on right knee and glass in left hand. With dog by right foot. Coloured in Manganese and green.

9. Judy Bland – Figure holding large jug in lap with both hands.

10. Brighton Museum – Figure holding jug in right hand, nothing in left.

11. Sold Bute Collection Auction, Christies, July 1996 – Cream ware Toby sitting holding a posy in right hand and glass(?) in right (missing). 6", blue coat and breeches. Sold for **£4950** with buyer's premium.

12. Sold Bute Collection Auction, Christies, July 1996 – Cream ware Toper sitting holding jug on right knee with right hand and glass in left. Green coat. 6¼" high. Sold for **£4950** with buyer's premium.

The Farrier

1. Stoke on Trent Museum – On the figure's knees is an apron upon which are resting pincers. In his left hand is a raised glass. In his right and resting on right knee is a jug. 6¼".

2. Sold Sotheby's February 1989, £17000/$25500, Alistair Samson – Same as (1) above.

3. Shown in *Early English Figure Pottery* **by Sir Harold Mackintosh, 1938** – Rodney Jug. Holding glass in left hand and large jug in right on right. Apron on knees. Complete with hat crown.

4. Olympia Antiques Fair, 1996 – Holding jug on right knee and glass in left hand, apron on knees, minus hat crown. This was stolen from the Olympia Antiques Fair on 3 June 1996 and and to date has not been found.

'The Farrier' sold at Sothebys, London, February 1989 for £17000.

The Tailor (The figure is ironing)

1. Captain R. K. Price collection from the Frank Falkner collection – Rodney Jug. Jug down by left leg. 11¾".

2. Captain R. K. Price collection – Bought from antiques dealer Mrs Curzon of Buxton. Jug down by right leg. 6¼".

3. Sold Sotheby's August, 27 1977, £2000/$3000 – Large jug in front of legs.

The Viola Da Gamba Player

1. Lord Mackintosh collection. Sold Sotheby's May 1967 from the Stacey Hooker collection – Playing instrument resting between his legs. Coat and instrument blue. 7¼". Bought by Manheim, **£350/$525**.

2. Burnap collection, Kansas City, Mo, USA – Viola De Gamba missing.

There is mention of a 'Cobbler' jug but I think this is a Farrier as both these tradesmen would have worn an apron and used pincers.

The Drummer

A Toby Jug similar to the 'Fiddler' but playing a drum held between his knees decorated in olive green and muddy brown colours. Height, 7½", whereabouts unknown, but seen as a picture in Collection of Early English Pottery — Part 4 compiled by Jonathan Horne.

The Sportsman

He is holding a jug on his right knee, glass (?missing) in his left hand, gun at his right side, dog between legs. 6¼" high. Sold at the Bute Collection sale, Christie's, July 1996 for **£6325** with buyers premium.

The Drummer, very rare.

CHAPTER SIX

The Female Tobies

The female Toby is not produced in anything like the numbers of her male counterpart, but where she is enshrined in the name of Toby she makes an interesting addition to any collection. In keeping with the tradition of the Toby she displays nothing of the beauty and finesse of the colourful fine china women so often produced over the last few centuries by potters attempting to immortalise the youthful women of their age. Not for us this age of senti-mentality – the female Toper could drink as well as any man, and did. When placed side by side with him on the shelf we catch a realistic glimpse of middle-aged men and women drinking to happiness in one of the few real solaces of the time in which they lived. She may also come in the form of a Snuff Taker, and in keeping with this tradition, the expression on her face is anything but a romantic one!

Female Toby Jugs are rare in that only eight different female characters are known to the author from the Georgian and Victorian eras, but of these characters two were so mass produced that they are still common today: 'Judy' and 'The Lady Toper'.

A portrait of Martha Gunn and the Prince of Wales, original in possession of HM the Queen.

Martha Gunn

Colour picture on pages 78 and 79

Martha Gunn was in many ways the lady of them all, so I will spend a little time describing her. She is probably the only person whose notoriety is due entirely to the fact that her character and occupation was depicted in the form of a Toby Jug. Had it not been for her portrayal in this form it is doubtful she would ever have been remembered.

In the Brighton Journal, 5 April 1780, the following advertisement appeared:

'To all bathers for the past 30 years, this is to acquaint the nobility, gentry and others resorting to Brightelmstone that Martha Gunn continues to bathe the ladies as usual, with James Johnson, a careful man with good horses, to conduct the machines in and out of the sea.'

Sea-bathing in the eighteenth century was not an easy business. The bathing machine was a small hut on cartwheels, and the services of a 'dipper' of the same sex was undertaken. It was Martha Gunn who bathed the ladies and she was described as 'the venerable Priestess of the Bath' by the Morning Herald. In 1806 the Herald paid the following tribute to her endeavours:

'The beach this morning was thronged with ladies, all anxious to make interest for a dip. The machines, of course, were in very great request, though none could be run into the ocean in consequence of the heavy swell, but remained stationary at the water's edge, from which Martha Gunn and her robust female assistants took their fair charges, closely enveloped in their partly coloured dresses, and gently held them to the breakers, which not quite so gently passed over them. The greatest novelty, however, that this part of the coast exhibited this morning, was a gentleman undressing himself on the beach, for the purpose of a ducking, in front of the town, attended by his lady, who sans diffidence, supplied him with napkins, and even assisted him in wiping the humid effects of his exercise from his brawny limbs, as he returned from the water to dress.'

In the same period Margaret Barton wrote:

There's plenty of dippers and jokers
And saltwater rigs for your fun
The King of them all is 'Old Smoaker'
And Queen of them, 'Old Martha Gunn'
The ladies walk out in the morn
To taste the saltwater breeze
They ask if the water is warm
Says Martha, "Yes Ma'am if you please."

Five years later, amongst the nobility was the Prince of Wales, George III's son, hence a fleur de lis in the Martha Gun's hat and the doggerel:

To Brighton came he
Came George III's son
To be dipped in the sea
By famed Martha Gunn.

The Prince of Wales first went to Brighton in 1785 aged 23 years and in that year Martha Gunn was 59. One cannot imagine why the rakish young Prince was being bathed by a 59 year old woman who would usually bathed ladies, but must have made an exception for the Prince.

The *Staffordshire Advertiser*, on 6 May 1815 printed her obituary: 'On Monday last, in the 89th year of her age, at Brighton, that well-known and esteemed character, as a bather, Martha Gunn of that town. She died on 2 May, 1815 aged 88 years and is buried in St. Nicholas' Churchyard.'

It is said that the female Toby Jug was modelled for Ralph Wood II probably by Voyez from an engraving. The print illustrated on page 59 is by John Russell — owned by the Queen — and hangs in Buckingham Palace along with its companion painting of 'Old Smoker' painted in 1787 and shows Martha Gunn holding the Prince of Wales aged about three years and about to put him in the sea.

But as mentioned before, the Prince of Wales was 23 when he first came to Brighton or Brightelmstone as it was then known. So the whole picture is nonsense or, shall we say, 'Artistic Licence'. Nevertheless both 'Prinny' and Martha Gunn accepted it. It was all good prestige for Martha Gunn, a rough tough beach attendant of the time, who lived in a fisherman's cottage in East Street, which is now occupied by Al Forno's Restaurant.

Recently, whilst standing in front of the giant range in the vast kitchen of the Brighton Pavilion, Philip Vainker of the Brighton Museum told me of the time when Martha Gunn, because of her familiarity with the Prince, was allowed into the kitchen. On this occasion she was observed to steal and conceal under her apron a lump of butter. The cook engaged her in conversation for some time in front of the range, where by the heat melted the butter down the front of her clothes, much to her consternation. It is said she was given a small stipend by the Prince and probably contributed to the headstone on her grave.

There is one other print of Martha Gunn taken shortly before her death, wearing the same mobcap under a bonnet.

This then is the story behind the character. She is depicted in the Toby Jug as a smiling female figure wearing a dress decorated with floral sprigs with smocking on the bodice, over which is an apron. On her head she wears a mob cap with a large brimmed hat on top (which is wider at the sides than at the front and back). The removable crown of the hat is like that of a bowler hat, but it is rare to find this still intact. Often omitted from the front of the brim is a relief of the Prince of Wales feathers, which are placed there in order to commemorate her bathing of the Royal personage in 1785. Prior to this date one would think that Martha Gunn would not have been a famous enough personage for the Woods, 300 miles away in Burslem, to have made a jug in her likeness. Also many which appear to be later jugs are lacking the Prince of Wales feathers. Maybe they were omitted purely for economy. In her right hand she holds what appears to be a flask of gin and in her left hand a glass.

The jug was possibly made by Ralph Wood II in running glazes, and in enamel colours c1790. Other potters were producing Martha around 1800. Oldfield and Co. of Brampton, Derbyshire also made Martha Gunn jugs in white stoneware c1833-88, but these are not very impressive. Wood and Son of Burslem made a limited edition of 1000 in 1973, 11" high and in enamel colours. See also Beswick under Twentieth Century Tobies.

It would be interesting to know who was the first to name this jug Martha Gunn. But anyone knowing her story could give her no other name as she wears Prince of Wales feathers in her hat. The earliest writing I can find about her is in *The Connoisseur* of November 1909, where Frank Falkner is describing the George Stoner collection of pottery by the Ralph Woods of Staffordshire.

He describes the jug as follows: As representing a comely though slightly anxious looking middle aged lady'. A very rare model indeed and an excellent piece of potting,

To the
Memory of Stephen Gunn
Who died 4th of Sept. 1813
aged 79 years.
Also Martha Wife of
Stephen Gunn
Who was particularly distinguished as a
Bather of this town, nearly 70 years.
She died 2nd of May 1815
Aged 88 years.
Also Friend, their son, who died
1st of Nov 1784 aged 22 years.
Also Elizabeth B.L. their daughter
who also died 2nd of Oct. 1797 aged 30 years.
Also Martha their daughter
who died 27th July 1789 aged 30
Also Thomas B.L. their son
Who died 5th of May 1798 aged 37 years.

Martha Gunn's grave can still be visited today. Her headstone, which is surrounded by iron railings, reads as above.

this specimen is decorated in coloured glazes, the writer knows an example of the lady decorated in enamel colours.' This is probably the jug illustrated (on page 78), impressed with No. 13, one of the unlisted Ralph Wood mould numbers, compiled by Frank Falkner in the above mentioned article. Of the listed numbers between 169, a total of 88 are missing, 13 being one of them. Only three were Toby Jugs, all the rest were figures.

The first actual naming of the jug as Martha Gunn that I can find is by Cyril Andrade who placed an advertisement in *The Connoisseur* of November 1919.

There have been few recorded in coloured glazes, one was sold in Christies Auction Rooms on 10 May 1918. The jug was originally bought in Ireland and given to a friend as a Christmas present. This friend being a collector knew it was valuable and advised his friend of the fact, who put it into the auction rooms. On the day of the sale he called into Christies to reduce the reserve that had been set at £60/$90 to £20/$30. The jug was finally knocked down at 600 guineas to Cyril Andrade a dealer of St James'.

The story goes that he and another dealer were commissioned to bid for this jug on behalf of a wealthy collector, said to have been Captain R.K. Price, who forgot that he commissioned two bidders on his behalf, consequently they bid against each other. R.K. Price had an identical Martha Gunn in his collection, also other Tobies that were sold at this sale. So the evidence points to he being the purchaser. It is interesting to note here that in 1987 I made contact with Captain Price's daughter, Venice P, who thought the mysterious purchaser was not her father, who she thought, always bid himself at auction. R.K. Price was born in 1870 and Harold Mackintosh as a friend and a fellow collector, frequented his home at Akeley Wood, Bucks, prior to his (R.K. Price) death in 1927.

Above: House in East Street, Brighton where Martha Gunn lived, and below the Commemorative plaque.

A Martha Gunn jug was made in Whieldon type mottled glazes, showing that the potter had a great sense of humour, for our bathing lady is sporting high arched eyebrows and a flamboyant moustache. The jug is lacking the hat. This is the only one recorded (*see colour picture page 78*).

Another very rare Martha Gunn, the only one so far recorded, is a Pratt type 11" high with a basket of oranges between her feet. Her dress is off white with dashes of blue, yellow and green all over (typical Pratt colours). In her right hand she holds the usual bottle and glass in left, mobcap and yellow shawl (*see colour picture page 78*).

The Martha Gunn jug sometimes may be found with a jug in place of the bottle held in Martha's right hand. These appear to be less common than the former, always in enamel colours and early nineteenth century. Also on some jugs a cat may be found between her feet.

I have in my possession an enamelled Martha Gunn holding a jug in her right hand and she has blue eyes. This is the only blue eyed Toby I have seen. It is said that figurines had brown eyes up to 1800 and blue after this date. This jug would be about 1820. Ralph Wood type c£1000/$1500, other early ones £500/$750+. Late reproductions under £100/$150.

Another very unusual Martha Gunn shows Martha smoking a shortened stem clay pipe held in he left side of her mouth and her tongue is sticking out of the right side of her mouth. Another unusual feature is that the Prince of Wales Feathers, instead of being on the front side of her hat brim, they are fixed on the top edge. Pratt ware c1790 (*colour picture on page 78*).

On late eighteenth and early nineteenth century jugs, Martha Gun is always shown sitting on a capstan, whether she did in real life while waiting for customers, or it is poetic licence to show her association with the sea shore it is not known.

Drunken Sal

Drunken Sal is wearing eighteenth century dress and a large brimmed hat, typical of many Hogarth prints, representing the gin drinking women of the time. The picture on page 79 shows Sal wearing a long white dress with a red, blue and green floral design which has been patched in ten places as denoted by the black stitching. She wears a white mob cap which is trimmed with black lace and on top of this is a large brimmed hat, the underside of which is yellow and trimmed with garlands of flowers. She has a torn blue shawl around her shoulders and black shoes. This is a very large jug probably only made by Davenport, dated around 1830. The bases are occasionally impressed with the Davenport mark, anchor and date numerals.

The jug depicts what can only be described as a sluttish leering woman sitting on a tree stump from which a branch rises upwards and forms the handle. From the base to the top of the hat brim the jug measures 12¼" and the base is 8" by 6¼". She holds a glass in her left hand and a clay pipe in her right, with a semblance of smoke billowing out (the pipe being moulded in with the body and the smoke being represented on her dress).

There is a much smaller version of this jug in all over white glaze. 'The Drunken Sal' comes up in English pottery sales far less frequently than 'Martha Gunn' and is beginning to catch up on price. Sold 1989, £750/$1125.

The Female Snuff Taker

Whilst the 'Male Snuff Taker' is the commonest of Toby Jugs, his female counterpart is fairly rare. The jug was probably made at Portobello c1845, and is decorated in typical hard bright enamel colours. It shows the Portobello characteristic of the use of maroon and large green vine leaves on the base.

These jugs are thickly potted but with quite good facial modelling which has a bluish tinge welling in the creases, but the harshness of the colours, typical of so late a Toby Jug, is not particularly attractive, and neither, judging from the expression on the woman's face, is the snuff she takes! £200/$300+.

There is a another lady Snuff Taker (maybe she is 'Judy') sitting and wearing long skirts with her apron gathered up around her waist. She wears a type of mob cap tied underneath her chin, on top of which is a tricorn hat. This too is a little encountered Toby Jug, only two recorded, c1830 (*see colour picture page 80*).

One very rare lady Snuff Taker is in the form of 'The Gin Woman' but is taking snuff. Only one has been recorded. *Colour picture on page 80.*

See also under Rockingham.

Two Lady Snuff Takers standing. Left: maker unknown; right Portobello.

The Gin Woman

This jug depicts a standing woman wearing the clothes which were fashionable around 1840, consisting of a crinoline skirt with apron which reaches to half-way down the calf of her legs. This was the common mode of dress for Cockney women at the time (*see colour picture on page 79*).

Both arms are moulded separate from the body of the figure and she holds a glass in her right hand and a bottle (a flask of gin) in the left. These Tobies were made in overglaze polychrome enamel colours, 8¾" high. Another quite rare version is a very finely modelled piece in pale blue overglaze enamel, standing 9½" high. They were more commonly made in Rockingham brown treacle glaze, about 8" high. A fourth version is an 8" high copper lustre model with white glazed face, hands and bottle. All were probably made c1840-50. £200/$300+.

A rare model may be found in Mersham Ware, late 19th century (*see colour picture on page 79*).

The Hurdy Gurdy Player

This must be the rarest of all the female Toby Jugs and like the 'Lady with the Fan', has a degree of refinement about her that the others lack.

This is a Staffordshire jug c1785, 8¼" high. It is modelled as a seated lady wearing a brown hat, yellow bodice and grey skirt, playing a Hurdy Gurdy. She has a monkey at her side playing a violin and the handle is in the form of a green dolphin on a rockwork base. Only one so far has been recorded. Value: £1000/$1500+.

Judy

Colour picture on page 73.

The wife of Punch. The two were first made by William Machin of Hanley, in 1889. On the underside of the original jug are incised, in ¼" numerals, 139844. Machin went out of business in 1911 and the original moulds were possibly acquired by William Kent, who continued to produce them, as late as 1962 in numbers 381 (Punch) and 382 (Judy). Judy originally had a removable hat crown, which is usually missing, probably as a result of the ease with which it can be damaged. This jug is quite common.

In 1924 Devonmoor made a Judy wearing a yellow dress with vertical and horizontal blue lines. On the front of dress sometimes is written 'Cheddar', made for that Somerset town 8¼", high marked 'Made in England'. Value: £70/$105+.

Judy & Punch. Maker unknown.

See also 'The Lady Snuff Taker'.

The Lady with the Fan

Colour picture on page 80.

A female Toby standing 11¼" high, made by Minton of Stoke-on-Trent in 1873. The standing lady with her hand across her breast holds a fan and has long hair dangling down her back, forming the handle of the jug. It was made as a companion to the 'Barrister Toby'. It was sold Sothebys Billingshurst, January 1999 for £500/$850

See 'Barrister' for colour variations.

The Lady Toper

Colour picture on page 98.

A name given to another female Toby Jug. She has a pleasant smile on her face, no doubt in contemplation of the benefits of her lovingly clutched drink, held in both hands. This jug was probably first made in Derbyshire majolicaware, it having a glaze running down the figure in yellow and green. If it is a Derbyshire majolicaware jug, Sharpe Brothers & Co were probably the makers, in Swadlincote, c1880. The polychrome model was probably made by William Kent of Burslem at the end of the nineteenth century and was still in the catalogue as late as 1962.

The models of this jug tend to be quite poor, but some of the majolica ones are very nice quality. Value: £50/$75

Lady and Man Topers by Sharpe Bros & Co c1880. Majolicaware.

Lady with Bag, Umbrella and Pig

Colour picture on page 80.

This jug has an all over green glaze. It shows a woman holding a Gladstone bag in her left hand with an umbrella in her right and under her right arm is a pig. The mark is a garter, on the border of which is 'Old London Ware' and in the centre a monogram 'G.R.M.' c 1880. Quite rare as I have not seen another. Value: under £100/$150

CHAPTER NINE

Twentieth Century Toby Jugs

The development of Toby Jugs after 1900 has followed a similar pattern to that of the earlier period. Once again we have a few Tobies of high quality and many of a poorer quality. There are still problems of identifying makers but thankfully these are confined to the poorer end of the range of Tobies. The Ordinary Toby as well as several other Toby characters continued to be produced after 1900, some of these as clever fakes of the original and others as more honest representations of popular designs. Many of these proved to be very desirable and these jugs are much sought after by collectors.

It was in the 1920s and 1930s that the twentieth century revival of Toby Jugs as a quality production item took place. Thanks to the commercial success of jugs produced by pottery manufacturers such as Doulton and Wilkinson Ltd, there was an upsurge in the production of jugs by other potters. Sadly, as we have come to expect with Toby Jugs, not all of these were up to the standard of Doulton and Wilkinson. Many new variations in size, shape and function were introduced, several of which proved very popular, particularly crested ware, miniatures and character jugs.

The production of other Toby items come under a miscellaneous group which is largely comprised of utility items that are in fact converted and contorted versions of the Ordinary Toby. Ranging from teapots and cream jugs to tobacco jars they were no doubt introduced because of the commercial success of Toby Jugs. Apart from those by potters such as Doulton and Beswick, they are in the main unmarked and very little information is known as production records are not available.

The Toby Jug has undergone further development with the introduction of the 'cousin' of the Toby Jug, the character jug. The most notable of this type is that produced by Royal Doulton. A character jug portrays the head and shoulders of its chosen subject as opposed to the full body of a Toby Jug. Whilst to many Toby collectors these represent a travesty of the real thing they are nevertheless extremely popular in their own right.

Throughout this century there has been a great expansion in the characters portrayed by Toby Jugs, from working tradesman of all sorts to religious characters such as Monks, Friars and Cardinals. Recent history has provided several new characters.

The most often portrayed figure in Toby form this century is undoubtedly Sir Winston Churchill, who was first represented in 1927. This jug by W. H. Goss proved to be the first of many which portray the man at various stages of his great political career. Other distinguished politicians such as Lloyd George have also been modelled.

The characters of Charles Dickens have proved very popular with Toby producers this century, as have the characters popularised by Shakespeare.

There have even been several individuals who for one reason or another have specifically commissioned Toby Jug likenesses of themselves to be produced. We will look at some of these later.

Twentieth Century Potteries who have made Toby Jugs

Cliff Adkins	Carlton	Hancock Corfield &	Roddy Ware	Thorley
Allerton	Cooper & Co	Walker	Romsby Pottery	Thornly
Arcadian	Cooper Clayton	Holkham Pottery	Royal Winton	Torquay Pottery
Artone	Copeland Late Spode	James Green & Nephew	Royal Torquay	Wade
Ashted	Crown Staffordshire	Keele Street Pottery	Royal Worcester	Wain (Melba Ware)
Ault	Dartmouth Pottery Ltd	Kelsboro Ware	Sandland	Wedgwood
Avon	Denton	Kent (Old Staffordshire)	Savoy	Wedgwood & Co
Bairstow Manor Pottery	Devon Tors (Bovey	Kevin Francis Ceramics	J. Shaw & Sons	Wilkinson Ltd (Newport
Ltd	Tracey)	Roy Kirkham Pottery	Shaw & Copestake	Pottery)
Beswick	Devonmoor	Kirkland	(Sylvac)	Willow Art & Willow
Bilks Rawlings & Co	Doulton	Lancaster	Shelly China	China
Blakeney Art Pottery	Empire	Lord Nelson Pottery	Shorter & Sons	Wood & Sons
Arthur Bower	Falbord ware	Martin Ware	Spencer & Stevenson	Wood, Tony (Studio 82)
Branham	Fielding (Crown Devon)	Melwood	(Royal Stuart) 1960	Wood, Arthur
Burgess & Leigh	Floral China	Old Ellgreave Pottery	onwards	Watcombe
Burleigh	Franklin Porcelain	P & J Meredith	Staffordshire Fine	
Burlington Ware	W. H. Goss	Paragon	Ceramics	
Cambrian Pottery	Grafton	Ridgways	Sterling	

Early Jugs up to c1850
Fiddler/Midshipmite/Rodney

Fiddler £5000+.

Lord Rodney mug, 1782.

Sailor with Bottle, 18th century, £3000+.

Tailor – Rodney £10,000+.

Rodney Jug, sold at Phillips in 1989 and centre after restoration using a cast taken from another Rodney jug, and right, inscription on base.

Very Rare No Base Toby, c1780, Ordinary, £3000+.

From left: Tailor, second and fourth Fiddlers; third from left, Beswick Fiddler.

The Nightwatchman, Rev George Whitfield Jug.

Ordinary Toby Types

Ordinary, c1780 £700+.

Ordinary, c1780, £600+.

Ordinary, c1780, £800+.

Ordinary, c1780, £800+.

Ordinary Ralph Wood type, 1780, £600+.

Ordinary Ralph Wood type, c1780, (raised glass) £800+.

Ordinary, Ralph Wood type, 1780, £700+.

Ordinary stepped base, c1780. Rare, original hat crown £800+.

Ordinary, 'Windmill' on small jug, Neal and Co, 1780, £600+.

Ordinary Raised Glass, 1780, £800+.

Ordinary c1790 from the collection of Captain R. K. Price, £700+.

Ordinary c1790, £600+.

Ordinary 1790 £600+.

Ordinary, on small jug, 'Mild Ale', 1790, £600+.

Ordinary, c1790-1800 £500+.

Ordinary c1790 Blue and White, £800+.

Ordinary, 1790, Pratt type, £600+.

Ordinary, 1790, Pratt Type, £600+.

Ordinary, Pratt Type, 1790, £600+.

Ordinary, Pratt Type, 1790, £500+.

Ordinary, c1790, Success to our wooden walls on small jug, £600+.

Ordinary, around base 'Robt & Ann Wagstaff, 1793'.

Ordinary, 1794-1820, made by Hollins, 12½", £1000+.

Ordinary, on small Jug 'Crispin and Crispinas 1798' £600+.

Ordinary 18th century with double base, £700+.

Ordinary with stem of pipe downwards, 1790, £700+.

Ordinary on high base, 18th century, £1000+.

Pratt Ordinary, with very rare handle, 18th century, 6¾" high, £300+.

Ordinary, 1800, £500+.

Ordinary, c1800, £600+.

Ordinary holding large jug, c1800, £300+.

Ordinary, c1800, £500+.

Ordinary, c1800, £500+.

Ordinary Pratt Type, c1800, £500+.

Ordinary Pratt Type, c1800, £500+.

Ordinary c1800 "Stingo" on small jug, £300+.

Ordinary, probably York-shire, c1800, £300+.

Ordinary (note hands), c1800, £600+.

Ordinary holding large jug in right hand and large pipe in left, probably Yorkshire, c1800, £500+.

Ordinary Pratt type c1800.

Stone Ware, Ordinary, by Oldfield & Co, 19th century, and right: back view, £400+.

Ordinary 'Ale' on small jug, c1820 £800+.

Ordinary, holding small jug, c1800, £600+.

Ordinary, 1820, with pink lustre coat, £300+.

Standing Toby with an unusual dolphin handle, c1820. The only one recorded.

Ordinary, looks like Lionel Barrymore could be Portuguese, 11" high, £600+.

Snuff Taker, type boy holding jug in place of snuff box, c1820, £300.

Ordinary with document history 1825, £300+.

Ordinary in stoneware, c1830 marked Bramton.

Pink lustre coat Ordinary with open mouth and 1¾" hole in base, 1830, £600+.

Stoneware Ordinary holding white pipe, impressed 'Pearson & Co, Whittington Moore, c1805-1879', £300+.

Ordinary 'Black Man' probably Portobello Ware. 1830, £300+.

Standing 'Black Man' Portobello Ware, 1830 £200+.

Black Man 19th Century £200+.

Bottle Toby 18th Century £2000+.

Ordinary, holding Bottle and Goblet, probably Yorkshire, 1800, £500+.

Ordinary holding Bottle and Goblet, probably Yorkshire, 1800, £500+.

Sailor with Bottle, 18th century, £3000+.

The Bargeman, £4000+.

The Coachman, c1780, £1000+.

Coachman, 19th Century, Ordinary £400+.

Convict, 18th century, £800+.

The Collier 1790 £800+.

Drunken Parson, c1820, £600+ each.

The Sinner, c1800, £2000+.

Unfrocked Parson, c1800, £2500+.

The Farmer, c1830, £1000+.

Three Hearty Good Fellows c1820, £400+ each.

'With my jug in one hand, and my pipe in the other', very rare Lakin & Pool, 1791-95.

Harty Good Fellow, 1820, £250+.

Harty Good Fellow, 1820 possibly by John Walton £250+.

Harty Good Fellow 1810 £400+.

Harty Good Fellow, 1820 £250+.

Earl Howe, 18th century, £2000+.

The Man on the Barrel (Earl Howe), 1800, £2000+, Ordinary

Long Face probably Ralph Wood, c1780 £1000+, Ordinary.

Long Face, 1780, £1000+, Ordinary

Prince Hal, c1785, £5000+.

The Postillion.

Punch, Portobello ware, c1840, £200+.

72

Punch and Judy, 19th century, £400+ the pair.

Right: Five tobies between 3"-4" high: Punch (£40+), Martha Gunn (£50+), three male tobies. (£30+, £20+, £20+).

Punch treacle glaze. £200+.

Ordinary Raised Glass, 1780, £800+.

Trafalgar Toby, 1815. £1500+. Inset: Victory Medallion on back of Trafalgar Toby.

Ordinary Yorkshire Raised Glass impressed crown on base, 1800, £800+.

Ordinary with Raised Glass, c1800, £600+.

Left: Ordinary Raised Glass, Silver Lustre, Yorkshire(?), 1820, £400+.

Right: Ordinary Raised Glass, Yorkshire, impressed crown, dog between feet, 1800, £400+.

Puzzle Jug Toby, c1800, £800+. Yorkshire?

Reading Toby, c1800, £1000+.

Ralph Wood Roman Nose, 18th century, £2000+.

Sailor with arm outstretched, pipe has been added. c1780, £2000+.

Sailor impressed on base 'Viscount Jarvis', c1790, £1000+.

Sailor, c1800, £1500+.

Three sailors, c1800, £3000+; £2000+; £1500+.

Large American Sailor, c1820, 11½", £600+. Left shows before restoration and right after.

Small American Sailor, 10¼", c1820. £500+.

Small American Sailor, c1820, 10¼", £500+.

Large American Sailor, c1820, 11½", £600+.

Sharp Face, probably Ralph Wood, c1780 £1000+, Ordinary.

The Shepherd c1790, £3000+.

Shield Toby (Ralph Wood), 18th century, £4000+.

Snuff Taker, c1830, £200+.

Snuff Taker 10¾" high, Portobello ware, c1830, £150+.

Snuff Taker, Portobello ware, c1840, £200+.

Snuff Taker, c1840, £150+.

Snuff Taker in stoneware c1840, £200+.

Snuff Taker, c1840 in brown Treacle Glaze, £50+.

Four Snuff Takers, tallest 5½", c1850, £40+ each.

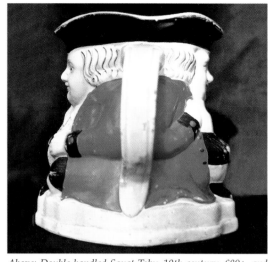

Above: Double handled Squat Toby, 19th century, £80+, and below sideways view.

Snuff Taker, marked on waistcoat initials "JH". 1842, £200+.

Soldier c1835, £200+.

The Squire, c1780, £1500+.

The Squire, Ralph Wood type, c1780, £1200+.

William Kent Squire moulds.

Ordinary with step base, c1800. £500+.

Step Toby, c1800, Ordinary, £600+.

Step Toby, c1800, Ordinary, £600+.

Step Toby, c1800, Ordinary, £500+.

Step Toby, c1800, Ordinary, £500+.

The Thin Boy, c1780, £3000+.

Three Thin Man, £2000+ each.

The Thin Man, c1780, £2000+.

Tipsy Man, sold at Sotheby's Scotland, 1990 £16,500 with buyer's premium.

Tythe Pig Parson c1780, £4000+.

Tythe Pig Parson, c1780, £4000+.

Tythe Pig Parson, 19th century, £4000+.

Village Idiot, c1790, £1700+.

The Welshman, £9000.

Wineskin Toby, c1800, £1000.

Brown Stoneware jug by Pearson & Co, mid 19th century. £200.

Female Tobies

Martha Gunn –

the inspiration for

the rest

Pratt ware Martha Gunn with Basket of oranges, c1800. The only one recorded. £1000+.

Martha Gunn impressed No. 13, John Wood (?) 1780, £1000.

Matha Gunn, Pratt ware, c1790, £800 +.

Martha Gunn Smoking Pipe with tongue out, c1790, £1000.

Martha Gunn sporting moustache, hat broken off, c1790, very rare, £1000.

Three Martha Gunns, all c1790 from left: Pratt ware, Ralph Wood (?) and Pearlware. Value £1000+ each.

Martha Gunn with Jug, c1810, £700.

Martha Gunn with Jug, c1810, £700.

Three Martha Gunn Tobies, c1810 £800+ each.

Martha Gunn, impressed Oldfield & Co, c1840, £600.

Drunken Sal by Davenport, c1850, £1000.

Rare Gin Woman, c1840, £600.

Measham Ware Gin Woman, late 19th century, £300. The only one recorded

Three Gin Women, c1840, £300 each.

Lady with Bag, Umbrella and Pig, c1880, £100.

Lady with the Fan, Minton with silver and base rim. Hallmarked for 1875.

Negro Slave Toby, c1850, £600.

Lady standing Snuff Taker, c1830, £200.

Lady Seated Snuff Taker, c1830, £500+.

Lady Snuff Taker, very rare, c1845, £400. Gin Woman type but a snuff taker.

Pair of Rockingham(?) Snuff Takers, c1840; £400.

CHAPTER TEN

Twentieth Century Potters

Cliff Adkins

Colour picture on page 108.
Cliff Adkins of Mashfield near Chippenham, Wiltshire started making Tobies as recently as 1998 with his first called Sleeping Toby. It is 8" high and is very light in weight and is different, with mice running up Tobies back and feet. **Retail price £100/$170.**

Allerton

Colour picture on page 99.
Charles Allerton and Sons potted in Staffordshire between 1831 and 1942, so their products are spread equally over both the nineteenth and twentieth century. The mark found on these jugs is often 'Allerton est 1831' which confuses some people to think that the jug they possess is of a date near to

Sleeping Toby by Cliff Adkins.

1831. However, in 1891 the word 'England' was added so any jug bearing this is certainly not early work. Allerton Tobies are 'Snuff Takers' or 'The Ordinary' types usually with blue coats. All colours are in bright enamels with lustre decoration and the modelling is rather poor. Some Allerton jugs were made for the American market marked underneath 'Made in England for the Scottish village Glendale, California'. These are not particularly valuable £20-£40/$30-$60.

Ashtead Potteries

This pottery was formed after the First World War in the early 1920s under the patronage of the Queen Mother who was then the Duchess of York to give work to wounded soldiers.

Mainly produced for the American market in the 1920s these Tobies in cream, portray a range of historical characters including such as 'Lloyd George', 'Baldwin' and 'Benjamin Franklin'.

A similar group of 'political' jugs may have been produced, probably around 1925. These were 'Earl Lloyd George', 'Sir Harry Lauder', 'Earl Baldwin', 'Ramsey Macdonald' and 'Lord Asquith'. All of these subjects are seated, 6" high and well modelled in subdued enamel colours. The only marks on them are raised numerals on the base, about ½" in size. 'Macdonald' bears the number 452 and 'Earl Baldwin' 451. The potter of these also made a male and a female Toby in the same fashion as the above group. *See also under Advertising Tobies Johnny Walker.* **Value: £20-£140/$30-$210**

A series of Toby Jugs from Ashtead Potteries modelled by Percy Metcalfe. From left: Benjamin Franklin; Lloyd George; Lord Hailsham; S. M. Bruce and Stanley Baldwin

Bairstow Manor Pottery Ltd

Bairstow Manor Pottery of Blackhorse Lane, Hanley, Stoke-on-Trent are making Tobies, mainly using the William Kent moulds.

Beswick Tobies

Colour picture on pages 103, 118.

As a result of the recent growth in interest in Beswick items generally, the Tobies and character jugs are now rising in value and collectability. Produced in the 1930s they are of appeal to Beswick collectors and Toby collectors alike.

The most interesting of the Beswick Tobies is the Midshipman (Fiddler), a very finely modelled and decorated jug. Apart from the one by F. Stoner (see under Fiddler jug), the only one believed to have been made in the past 200 years, although I have seen a poorly modelled little 'Fiddler' jug unmarked. Winston Churchill 7" Reg No 931 1941-54 £200/$300; Toby Phillpot 8" Reg No 1110 1948-69 £120/$180; Toby Holding Glass 5½" Reg No 1111 1948-69 £75/$110; Midshipman (Fiddler) 5¼" Reg No 1112 1948-69 £150/$225; Martha Gunn 3½" Reg No 1113 1948-69 £150/$225; Toby Sitting on Barrel 3½" Reg No 1114 1948-60 £125/$185; Lord Mayor 8" Reg No 1741 1961-70 £100/$150 – Reintroduced 1985-87 *(See under Advertising Tobies)*

Bishop

See under Goss.

Branham

See under 'Black Man Toby'.

Burgess and Leigh

Colour picture on page 104.

They produced two different jugs portraying Winston Churchill in the 1940s. 1) Bulldog script . . . 'We shall defend every village, every town and every city'. 2) 'John Bull Churchill'. Value: £20-£40/$30-$60

Burleigh Tobies (Burgess and Leigh)

This pottery produced a range of Shakespearian and Dickens characters in the 1950s. These well made jugs range in height from 3" to 6" and were mainly produced for export although they are reasonably common in the UK. **Value: £20-£40/$30-$60**

Burlingtonware

'Burlingtonware' was a mark found on the products of J. Shaw of Tunstall 1931-63, who produced a range of relatively inexpensive jugs, particularly in the 1950s. All the jugs are over 6" in height, some up to 12" and the characters portrayed include the 'Sleeper', 'Singer', 'Captain Hook', 'John Bull' and 'Long John Silver'.

The 'Long John Silver' is a poorly modelled jug which is an injustice to one of the great characters in British literature. He is, as to be expected, standing on one leg with the aid of a crutch. He wears a long red or green coat and black tricorn hat with a yellow band around the brim. On his right shoulder is a parrot and in his right hand he holds a cutlass. Around his waist is a belt which has a pistol thrust through it. It is a common jug and can be bought for around £30. The others have a similar value. This jug was also made with a musical movement in base which makes it a little more expensive.

Also made was a table lamp in the form of an Ordinary Toby. 10" high and one slightly smaller. The domed hat crown is built into the brim with a ⅜" dia. hole to take the lamp holder and a 2" dia. hole in the base in order to secure same. **Value: £40-£60/$60-$90.**

In 1960 Burlingtonware moulds were sold to Staffordshire Fine Ceramics in Williamson Street, Tunstall.

Rev P. B 'Tubby' Clayton MC

Colour picture on page 106.

The founder of Toc H, a British fellowship of young men, the idea of which was first formed during the First World War in 1915, at Talbot House, Poperinghe, Belgium, and later as a Church Institute at the Guild Church in All Hallows, Barking by the Tower, London. He died in 1972.

There were only six Toby Jugs made, designed and modelled by Ken C. Speaks, two of which are shown below. The jug on the left shows Tubby Clayton holding a dog, because Ken Speaks informs me, Tubby always had a dog with him. Five of the six jugs shows him holding a dog.

The jug on the right shows him holding the Toc H lamp in his right hand. On the left pocket of his jacket is the Toc H badge. The Jugs are in underglazed Wheildon type coloured manganese and copper oxides. They stand 7" high and were made in 1959.

Copeland Spode

Colour picture on page 104.

Known to have produced a range of Tobies in 1947 and possibly into the 1950s, the most collectable being the 8½" Winston Churchill, seated and smoking a cigar. These jugs were decorated in bright blue and yellow colours, although some of them were issued in white because between 1945 and 1952 no coloured ware was permitted in Britain. This Toby figure is not very rare. Spode also made a Franklin D. Roosevelt which pairs with the Churchill jug. This Toby is quite rare. Both jugs were modelled by Eric Olsen. **Value: £50-£75/$75-$105.**

Crested Wares Tobies

In the 1880s Adolphus Goss, the son of a Stafford pottery manufacturer, came up with the novel idea of producing miniature porcelain items carrying individual town's coats of arms. These were sold as souvenirs to holiday makers. Other manufacturers soon followed and 'Crested ware' proved to be very popular.

The W.H. Goss factory moved its total output into this area and entered a sustained period of growth. The objects portrayed seemed to cover every conceivable subject from churches to antiques, but it was not until the 1930s that Toby Jugs were introduced in any quantity and range.

Crested Tobies are to be found ranging in size from miniatures at 1½" to larger versions of 4". Listed below are those Tobies that were either produced by Goss or by other makers on behalf of Goss. In all cases (apart from the odd female type) Ordinary Tobies were produced.

Other Crested Ware Tobies which are not produced by Goss are often judged by collectors as being inferior in value, in spite of the fact that many Goss Tobies were produced for Goss on their behalf. Apart from the Stratford Toby and the Churchill, all Goss Toby Jugs were made in the Thirties. Examples can be found varying in size from 1¾" to 6½". There are many other additional Crested Ware examples of Toby Jugs. These are very similar as many makers including Goss used the same manufacturers moulds. These range in size from miniatures at 1½" to others as high as 4" and are to be found in a range of colours.

W.H. Goss Toby Jugs

Colour picture on pages 102, 108.

Stratford on Avon Toby Jug (£70)/Basin; Churchill Toby Jug; inscribed on top hat: *'Any Odds-bar one thats me who kiss the Blarney Stone'.* This jug was also made with a black hat and no inscription. British Sailor (blue colouring). Miniatures (male and female). Ordinary Tobies. White glazed and crested. Multi coloured. Red Coat with verse (£100): *No tongue can tell / No heart can think / Oh how I love / A drop to drink.* One Arm Handle Toby. Female Toby.

The most impressive of the Goss Tobies is 6½" high in porcelain, showing his right arm sticking out holding a wooden club which is used as the jug's handle. The backstamp shows the usual Goshawk and was made c1930. Quite rare, value £150/$280.

There is another jug which is identical and is probably made from the same mould but there is no backstamp. It is painted mainly in black and blue but is unlikely to be made by Goss.

There is one other identical in design and colour but is 2⅛" higher made by Bishop c1930.

Other Crested Ware Toby Jugs

The more desirable specimens made by the heraldic china factories in Staffordshire between 1890 and 1940 were the coloured versions not bearing coats of arms. The crested varieties are less expensive and were produced in a multitude of different shapes for the collector. The majority of these delightful porcelain jugs are less than 4" high.

For further information please refer to *Crested China* by Sandy Andrews and *The Price Guide to Crested China* by Sandy Andrews and Nicholas Pine (Milestone Publications, Murray Road, Horndean, Hants). Arcadian; Ordinary; Sailor (fully coloured with rope handle; Black Boy Toby (fully coloured).

Carlton Ware

Ordinary Toby with verse. Many others to be found including a 3" high condiment set of mustard, salt and pepper, in colours of black, red, yellow and blue. They are marked with the Rd No. 738537 c1925. These are similar to the small Royal Worcester jugs. Value: under **£100/$150** for set of 3.

Grafton China

All fully coloured. Welsh Lady, John Bull, Irishman, Scotsman.

Savoy China

This factory has produced a range of fully coloured Toby Jugs without any crests on them. They are all about 2"-3" high.

Willow Art and Willow China

Is known to have produced several crested Tobies that are fully coloured, several of which were no doubt produced for Goss.

Crown Devon

See Fielding & Co.

Denton

Their mark is to be found on a range of miniature Dickens characters along with other characters such as Punch. All the jugs are around 3" in height and are quite collectable, although fairly reasonable to purchase.

Devonmoor

Colour picture on page 102.

This Devonshire pottery started in 1913 and discontinued a year later in 1914, probably due to the outbreak of the First World War. They started up again in 1922. They made Tobies in sizes from 1½" up to 24". They have a cat-like smiling face, with a pig tail hanging down over the left shoulder or down back. It would be interesting to collect a set of all the different sizes, as to date they are inexpensive, but for the 24" which is around **£1000/$1500+** (*see under Largest Toby*).

A 'Judy' was also made 8¼" high. Sometimes with 'Cheddar' written on front of dress (*see under 'Judy'*).

On the base of Devonmoor jugs sometimes is painted 'WMT. 1924' in maroon. These were decorated by Winifred Tapper who was one of the earliest painters at Devonmoor. She was trained by Mrs Hope and later went on to decorate Widecombe Fair character jugs. Also the initials R. E., D. E., H. J., C. P. and S. S. are found which are the initials of decorators.

Royal Torquay Pottery

Made Tobies on a rectangular base in seven sizes.

Devon Tors, Bovey Tracey

Made Tobies more squat than the others, with very shallow moulding.

Watcombe Toby

Dating from the 1950s with a bright turquoise slip coat. The Devonmoor Tobies had a white body, (the other Devon jugs are brown clay). Sometimes on the front place names such as 'Lands End' or 'Cheddar' are found, as they were sold as souvenirs. Devonmoor also made a condiment set consisting of salt, mustard and pepper approx 3" high, but is not common. (For most of the above I wish to thank Margaret Broderick of the Torquay Pottery Collection Society)

Doulton, Burslem

Colour picture on page 102.

Probably the most commercially successful Toby Jugs this century have been produced by Royal Doulton. Amongst collectors and dealers many of their withdrawals produce some quite startling prices, the world record price for a twentieth-Century Toby Jug being recorded for a Charlie Chaplin and a George Robey which sold for over $7000 dollars privately in America. Doulton Tobies are worth keeping, but production is insignificant in comparison to their massive character jug range.

Current Royal Doulton Tobies

Large	*Medium*	*Small*
Falstaff	Jolly Toby	Happy John
Happy John	Winston Churchill	Honest Measure
Hunstman		Falstaff
Sherlock Holmes		Winston Churchill
Sir Frances Drake		
Winston Churchill		

Discontinued Royal Doulton Tobies

These jugs were either produced as pilots or were only produced for a short time. Rarity is a far more important factor amongst these jugs than age alone. All of the Doulton Tobies listed below are worth far more than the average Victorian jug, despite being nearly 100 years younger. These jugs are very easy to identify by the Doulton backstamp and the style and quality of the modelling and colours.

Old Charley – large D6088	1939-1960	8¾"	D6030		Double XX	1939-1969	6½"
Old Charley – small D6319	1939-1960	5½"	D6069		The Squire	1950-1969	6"
Best is not too good	1939-1969	4½"	D6107				

The Dickens Seated Tobies Set

These were produced between 1938 and 1960 as part of a range of Dickens decorative items by Royal Doulton. The six seated Tobies are 4½" in height and were designed by Harry Fenton. They are very popular amongst Doulton collectors and they regularly sell for between £100/$150 and £130/$260. The set comprises:

Fat Boy; Mr Pickwick; Mr Micawber; Sam Weller; Captain Cuttle; Sairey Gamp.

George Robey

Colour picture on page 102.

This jug was produced by commission in 1926. The jug portrays the popular music hall artist George Robey who was known in his time as the Prime Minister of mirth. The jug is 10½" in height and has a detachable hat as a lid. 'George Robey' is etched on the front of the base. Market value: In 1985 this jug was selling for around £3500/$4250. One that was sold in auction in 1991 fetched £1000/$1500. I have one of these Tobies unmarked and I know of one other. These found their way out of the Doulton factory unfinished, not an unknown occurrence in the ceramics industry.

Charlie Chaplin

Colour picture on page 100.

Very similar in style to the George Robey Toby and was produced in 1918. It stands just over 11" high with a detachable bowler as a lid and carried the inscription 'Charlie' on its front. Market value £1500-£2000/$2200-$3000. Less than 10 are known.

Silver Rim Huntsman

Colour picture on page 102.

Is a variation of the Kingsware Huntsman jug that was introduced in 1910 at the Burslem studios. It has a distinct silver rim around the top which is hallmarked 1919. It is undoubtedly a pilot piece only one example having been uncovered and this sold at Phillips auctioneers for £200/$300 in 1980, a sum which would be considerably exceeded if it or another were to appear today.

The Cliff Cornell Toby Jug

These jugs were made in 1956 by private commission for the American industrialist Cliff Cornell. His likeness to Churchill and his fascination with the man, are borne out by the end product which is very similar to the Churchill Toby which Cornell specifically requested.

The jugs come in two sizes 9" and 5½", and in three colours, brown, blue and tan. The brown and blue version were produced in quantities of 500 each for the large size and 375 for the smaller size. The production run for the tan version is unknown but seems to be far less, being difficult to find and the most expensive to buy. The blue and brown versions sell at between £200-£250/$300-$375 for the large size and £150-£200/$225-$300 for the small.

Tom Bowling

Showing a man in the act of delivering a 'Wood' (bowling ball). He wears on his head a bowler hat (Derby), 11½", high modelled by Charles Vyse.

Doulton Burslem and Lambeth Studios

Although Doulton and Watts had produced a few Toby Jugs in the nineteenth century, it was not till the 1920s that Toby Jugs started to become a significant output of the company. These Toby Jugs, produced between 1910 and 1930, are a tribute to the skills of the designer Harry Simeon. The success of all future

Doulton Tobies was inspired by the early work of this designer. All of his work portrays stoneware Ordinary type Toby figures and some sitting astride stoneware barrels. Many were incorporated at Doulton's Lambeth factory into other objects such as ashtrays, tobacco jars and teapots.

Empire

Colour picture on page 98.

The Empire Porcelain Co, Empire Works, Stoke, Staffordshire started potting in 1896 and were still in business in 1963. The one Toby that I have seen is very similar to the Copeland Spode Jug pictured on page 98. It was probably made c1920.

I'm on the Black List

Colour picture on page 99.

A Toby only waist high, showing a man wearing a black coat, green waistcoat, yellow spotted scarf and a black high crowned hat on his head. In his right hand he is holding a white sign which reads 'I'm on the Black List'. It has been suggested that this represents an Irishman and the wording has some connection with Guinness. Other variations include "I'm banned from Blackpool' and 'I've been banned'. These were made in various sizes.

The jug stands 11" high and on the underside is marked 'Made in England, Rd No 476210', which is the registration year of 1906. Maker unknown and is moderately rare. **£50/$75+.**

I have seen one other holding the sign 'Recaerdo'.

Leonard Jarvis

Colour picture on page 105.

Little is known of Leonard Jarvis, but he is always referred to as a restorer. Without doubt this is one of the finest twentieth century Toby Jugs that has been made. Sir Winston Churchill was modelled by Leonard Jarvis in the fine translucent glazes of the Ralph Wood style. Its conception was inspired by Lord Mackintosh. It showed Churchill in his famous 'Victory' pose with the two fingers of his right hand raised. His left hand holds a palette and brushes, at his right foot is a pile of letters with an inkwell and quill pen on top, and there is a trowel at his left foot. We thus see Winston Churchill for his many attributes, as war leader, painter, brick layer and writer.

This Toby is 7" high and signed 'L. Jarvis'. It was made in a limited edition and it is also numbered, but the limit to the edition is not known. The going price in 1991 was **£800/$1200.** They were made with yellow and turquoise coats. At the Bute sale in 1996 one sold for **£1840/$3600** with buyers premium.

Lord Mackintosh

Colour picture on page 105.

This jug was made in a very limited edition in 1953, like the Winston Churchill jug in coloured glazes. Lady Gwynneth Mackintosh informs me that there was only a dozen or so potted and that they are all owned by members of the family.

The jugs stand 7½" high, some with a blue coat and some with green. On the left side of which is the Mackintosh coat of arms and on the other side the International Advertising Conference symbol. While on the knee breeches and shoes are the white rosettes of Yorkshire, in his left hand he holds a pipe and in his right a bust of John Wesley.

Lord Mackintosh of Halifax was the head of the Mackintosh Confectionery Company, was a renowned collector of early Staffordshire figures and Toby Jugs and instrumental in Leonard Jarvis making the Winston Churchill jug. He was a friend of Captain R.K. Price, another famous Toby collector in the first quarter of this century, who died in 1927. Lord Mackintosh died in December 1964.

William Kent (Old Staffordshire)

Colour picture on pages 99, 101, 102.

William Kent started producing figures and ornaments in Burslem from 1878. His original Toby moulds were obtained from William Machin. He went into partnership with John Parr in 1880 till 1894 and then carried on potting alone. After this his sons and then his grandson ran the pottery until 1962 when it was taken over by the Blakeney Art Pottery.

Right through the twentieth century up until 1962 the Kent pottery were producing Toby Jugs in overglaze colours in the style of the nineteenth century potters. These were mainly unmarked but in some cases there is the mark 'Old Staffordshire Ware England'.

The following models were produced:

Model	Reg No	Value	Model	Reg No	Value
The Ordinary	387	£100/$150	Jolly Miller	370	£100/$150
Hearty Good Fellow	373	£100/$150	John Bull	374	£100/$150
The Squire	380	£200/$300	Pickwick	391	£100/$150
Judy	382	£100/$150	Toby Teapot	366	£100/$150
Punch	381	£100/$150	Snuff Taker	390	£100/$150
Squat	368	£100/$150	Kneeling Toby	481	£100/$150
Night Watchman		£100/$150	Standing Pot Belly	481	£100/$150

Roy Kirkam Pottery

Colour picture on pages 107, 119.
See under Wedgwood & Co. A modern range of Tobies produced since the 1970s ranging in height from 5" to 7".

Martin Ware Toby

Sitting man with beard, 10" high. Marked 'Martin Ware London and Southall 11-1903'. The Martin Brothers also made a jug of a standing man shrouded in a cloak called the Monk jug.

The Motorist

Colour picture on page 100.
The name is mine. A most amusing jug in the human form and the most practical, owing to the rotundness of the figure.

The jug stands 8½" high and shows a man draped in a long brown leather overcoat, with only his toes of the right foot peeping out. His hands are in his pockets. Around his lower face up to his nose is a scarf which hangs down his back and forms the handle. He wears goggles, and a black coloured chauffeur's cap is on top of his head.

It has been suggested that it might represent Mr Toad of Toad Hall, from Wind in the Willows fame. On the base is an unreadable raised device incorporating an anchor and the numerals 4305. Maker unknown but c1920s. **Value: £100/$150**

Old Bill, The Gamekeeper, Poacher or Hunter

Colour picture on page 99.
Which of these titles this jug represents is hard to say. He looks very much like Bruce Bainsfathers' 'Old Bill' with his walrus moustache. But, Mr Reg Quaife, who owns the jug, contacted the Imperial War Museum and they thought not. In fact they didn't think it was a military figure at all and suggested the above names. They pointed out that 'Old Bill' was always depicted wearing a tin-hat and puttees, which is not correct, for there is a 'Carltonware' crested china figure, with the inscription 'Yours to a cinder, Old Bill'. He is shown wearing a balaclava.

There is also 'Old Bill Plate' showing him eating plum and apple jam out of a tin. He is wearing a peaked cap (peak to the front). Made by the Girls of Staffordshire during the winter 1917-18, Grimwades China.

The figure shows a seated man holding a jug on his right knee and glass in his left hand. On his right side is a square pouch and what could be a water or powder flask. Over his left shoulder is slung a rifle. On his head he wears a peaked cap with the peak facing the back.

The jug is 9⅜" high and probably made in England around 1917, but there are no makers marks.

Two have been recorded in all over white and two with blue hat and coat, light brown trousers, black shoes. The pouch, flask jug and glass are white. £150/$225.

Old Ellgreave Pottery, Burslem

Colour picture on page 108.

Paragon

Colour picture on page 104.
This company made at least a 'Punch and Judy' jug 2½" high c1939-49. Marked 'Paragon Fine China England by appointment to HM The Queen and HM Queen Mary'.

Sandland

These jugs sometimes marked 'Lancaster' portray an array of characters from Uncle Tom Cobbleigh to

Robin Hood. They come in four sizes, tiny, miniature and small; with the larger size often found with a silver rim. All the jugs were discontinued in 1968.

Shaw & Copestake Sylvac Staffordshire

At least three variations of small multi-coloured Tobies have been produced at this pottery.

Shelley

The Shelley pottery produced five different Toby Jugs at their Foley works at the turn of the twentieth century, ranging in height from 4" to 8". The first three were produced in 1899 in whiteware and multi-colouring. The remainder were made in 1911 as part of the Intarsio range. Standing 8" high they are characterised by their dark brown and green colouring. Since they are collected by both Shelley enthusiasts as well as Toby collectors their values are correspondingly far higher than they might bee. The Friar Tuck made £260/$390 plus commission at the Phillips auctioneer's Art Nouveau Decorative Arts & Studio Ceramics sale held on 13 June 1985. A similar value can be placed on the other four Shelley Tobies.

Of interest to the collector of miscellaneous Tobies are the Shelley Character teapots. One will however need a good bank balance as these teapots are very valuable. Made during 1900 they feature ordinary characters as well as several politicians including Lord Salisbury, Gladstone, Chamberlain and the South African politician Kruger. The modeller for all the teapots was Frederick Rhead. Some characters are found in a taller body as compared to the small body teapots. The value of these items has been increasingly rising with an auction price range of £200/$300 to £650/$975 given by the leading auction house in this area of collecting, Phillips of London.

Shorter & Son

Colour picture on pages 101, 105.
Since 1917, this company has made some forty Toby jugs including:

The Beefeater	Parson John	Gilbert and Sullivan Jugs
Pirate	John Bull	Toby plate
Guardsman	Fisherman	Toby Teapots (3 sizes)
Henry VIII	Flower Seller	Lady Pirate of Penzance 9½" high
Cavalier	Highwayman	Standing Toby 10¾" high
Chelsea Pensioner	King Nepture	Ordinary Toby 12½" high (*see Chapter 3*)

These jugs are becoming very collectable and some especially the Gilbert and Sullivan series fetch over **£400/$600.**

'Parson John' c1940 is identical to 'the Pickwick' seated Toby made by Sampson Smith and probably made from the same moulds. One 8" high Toby probably called 'Mac' or 'Scottie' has a musical movement in base which plays Auld Lang Syne.

Fourteen jugs modelled on characters from the Gilbert and Sullivan operas (*see colour picture page 105*): The Mikao; The Gondoliers; HMS Pinafore; The Pirates of Penzanace and the Yeoman of the Guard, came from an idea first conceived in 1939 and finally brought to fruition in the 1950s. They are said to be designed by Clarice Cliff. Betty Silvester modelled 'The Duchess of Plaza Toro', 'The Pirate King' and 'The Pirate Maid'. The D'Oyle Carte Opera Company gave permission for the costumes to be copied. These jugs may be found without the backstamp as some wholesalers requested them without the Shorter name.

Also in the mid 1980s a few Tobies including a 10½" high Ordinary were issued by somebody who owned the moulds for a short time and they were marked 'Rockingham' with a black script on underside of base.

Staffordshire Fine Ceramics

In 1960 Burlingtonware (J. Shaw) moulds were bought by Staffordshire Fine Ceramics of Tunstall, so some of these jugs might well appear under a new name. This company claims to be the most prolific makers of Toby Jugs in the world today. Amongst other Toby Jugs are:

Queen Elizabeth I	Collier	Customs Man	D'Artagnon
Queen Mary Tudor	Hornblower	Tall Storyer	Porthos
Queen Victoria	Squire	Will Shakespeare	Athos
King Henry VIII	Game Keeper	Smithy	Aramis
Touchstone	Pedler	Han	Poorman

Gaoler	Coachman	Inn Keeper	Beggarman
Toby	Lamp Lighter	Sweep	Thief
Nick	Snuffy		

Also a 22" high Falstaff which costs around **£1000/$1500.** But surely the most flamboyant Toby Jug made by Staffordshire Fine Ceramics, if not by anyone else for that matter, is the Abraham Lincoln jug with its 7" wing span eagle handle. The jug stands 11½" high depicting the President sitting in a chair, dressed in black. Over his left side is draped the American flag and at his right side a large scroll on which is written the Gettysburg address and at the back stands the Statue of Liberty. These jugs were specially made for American Embassies at a cost of about **£1200/$1800** each. *Colour picture on page 107.* The one illustrated is unfinished in as much that owing to imperfections in the second firing the jug was not completed and so it omits the writing on the scroll, the colours on the flag and all gilding that would have been on the completed jug. The jug was designed and modelled by Doctor Paul Sing who spent two years on the work. It was done just before the Statue of Liberty was restored in the 1980s. Up to June 1988 there had been approx. 60 jugs made, but the moulds are still intact.

In 1992 a Toby of Nigel Mansell, the racing driver was made.

F. Stoner

See under Fiddler Jug.

Wade

This pottery made a Toby for Charringtons Brewery. Identical to the one made by Doultons (see under Advertising Tobies).

Wain (Melba Ware)

Colour picture on page 105.

Wain produced a range of characters designed to compete with those produced by Royal Doulton. Although of a high quality they were withdrawn a few years after being introduced in the 1950s as they did not prove a commercial success. They range in size from 7½" to 12" high. Amongst other Tobies made: 'Cardinal Wolsey', 'Punch and Judy man', 'King Henry VIII', 'Shylock', 'Tale Teller'.

Wedgwood

Colour picture on page 104.

The only record of a Toby Jug produced by Wedgwood this century is known as the Elihu Yale Toby. This was produced for the Yale publishing association as part of its series of Wedgewood Yale Tableware in 1933. There were four colours, light brown, plain cream, blue and dark brown. The Toby was made in an unknown quantity and offered for sale at $4 each or 12 for $39. They infrequently turn up in the UK but a few have found their way back.

The jug was modelled by Professor Robert G Eberherd from a portrait of Elihu Yale painted in 1717 and owned by the Yale College since a bequest in 1789. On base is marked:

The Elihu Yale Toby.
Patent applied for
R.G.E. Sculp 1933
Wedgwood
Made in England.
IOB.33.

There is no record of Wedgwood ever making a Toby Jug in the eighteenth or nineteenth centuries.

Wedgwood & Co

Nightwatchman – *Colour picture on page 106.*

Bearing the raised marks 754 unicorn, Nightwatchman, England, under-glaze printing showing the head of a unicorn, 'Handpainted' Wedgwood & Co Ltd England Copyright.

This is a well modelled jug made c1895. Showing a little old man (free standing no base) dressed in a long brown coat, his hat is of the Beefeater type, in his right hand is held aloft a six sided lantern, in his left a rattle, his face is reminiscent of Bruce Bainsfathers 'Old Bill'. This 'Nightwatchman' 'The Night Watch' used to walk the streets during the hours of darkness calling our the hour of the clock. The jug stands 6½" high and 4¼" high. Also made: 'The Archbishop' no. 778, 'The Soldier', 'Knight of the Garter'. Wedgwood & Company (Ltd) Staffordshire potters operated the Unicorn and Pinnox works at Tunstall since 1860. The mark of this firm Wedgwood and Co. is often mistaken for that of the well known company of Josiah Wedgwood and Sons (Ltd). This firm does not include '& Co' in its marks. Wedgwood and Co. was formerly Podmore, Walker and Co. potting at Tunstall c1834-59. The name was changed to Enoch Wedgwood (Tunstall) Ltd.

Sometime, probably early this century, many of the moulds were sold to the Roy Kirkham Pottery, including the above mentioned 'Nightwatchman'. But it is interesting to note that the lantern held in the right hand is now moulded separately and attached to the hand by a metal ring. The mark is now in raised lettering, 754/1 Nightwatchman Made in England and stamped under the glaze in black Roy Kirkham Pottery Made in Staffordshire, handpainted. All the foregoing shows the continuing saga of one pottery selling out to another.

Wilkinson Ltd

Carruthers Gould Jugs
Colour picture on page 101.
One of the finest and most sensational group of Tobies in the twentieth century were the eleven jugs modelled as representations of the First World War Allied Commanders. These were designed by Sir F. Carruthers Gould and potted by Wilkinson Ltd of the Royal Staffordshire Potteries, retailed by Soanne and Smith Ltd of Oxford Street, London W1.

Sir Francis Carruthers Gould (known as FCG) was born in 1844 and died in 1920, being one of the most famous political cartoonists of his time, working mainly for *The Westminster Gazette*. Of many obituary notices, not one mentions his design of the eleven Wilkinson jugs, but this is probably the one thing he will be remembered for in the years to come.

There were eleven jugs potted between 1915 and 1919, issued in the following order:

Name	Entitled	Value
Lord Kitchener	Bitter for the Kaiser	£550-£775 / $825-$1150
This first jug was produced in a limited edition of 250		
Admiral Beatty	Dreadnought	£400-£550 / $600-$825
Field Marshall Haig	Push and Go	£400-£600 / $600-$900
Admiral Jellicoe	Hell Fire Jack	£400-£550 / $600-$825
Marshall Joffre	75mm Ce que joffre	£400-£600 / $600-$900
Lord French	French Pour Les Francais	£400-£550 / $600-$825
Rt. Hon. D. Lloyd George	Shellout	£400-£600 / $600-$900

Each of the above were produced in a limited edition of 350, the first two retailing at £2-12-6 each, the others at £2-2-0 each. They now sell for between **£300-£350 each.**

The remaining two were:

General Botha	Loyalty	£1800 / $2700

General Botha was produced as a limited edition of only 250 and is by far the rarest of these jugs to be found. The retail price was £3.30.

H.M. King George V	Pro Patria	£1000 / $1500

The King George V Toby was produced in a limited edition of 1000, but for some reason there are two variations of the jug. Some are fully coloured and others are all white. These retailed at £7.70/$11. The fully coloured version sells for three times the value of the plain white version, **c£700/$1050**. The set of 11 jugs were selling for around **£5000/$7500** in 1990.

It may have occurred to the reader that eleven is a strange number for a 'set' of figures. Winston Churchill may have been intended to make this number up, and it is suggested that he was the intended twelfth figure. The reason for his omission may have been that he fell out of favour over the 'Dardenelles' affair in 1915. He was certainly not a popular figure as Chancellor during Britain's Twenties slump, but he regained favour during and after World War II.

As Sir Carruthers Gould was no longer alive at that time, Clarice Cliff was given the design commission. But in spite of these claims it may be erroneous to make the connection because the

Tobies by Roy Kirkham, 1981. Top: Beadle, Friar Tuck, Town Crier. Bottom: Poor Man, Sweep.

Clarice Cliff version is at variance with the World War I set and was of course made to commemorate Churchill's activities in a different war.

Clarice Cliff's model of Winston Churchill bears the phrase, 'May God Defend The Right' on the front of the base. He is holding a warship in his hands and is dressed in uniform, sitting on a bulldog. The jug was potted by the Royal Staffordshire Pottery Co of Burslem. It is 11½" high and was issued in 1941. The current value of this jug is around (1990) **£1000/$1500**.

Clarice Cliff also designed a 'Mr Chamberlain' c1940, 12" high with 'Justice, peace, happiness and truth' on the base and around the same time a jug of Reginald J. Mitchell, designer of the Spitfire fighter plane (who was born in Stoke-on-Trent). The figure is dressed in a grey suit and trilby hat, seated on clouds modelled with three Spitfires. A metallic figure of mercury flies before him. The handle is modelled as a micrometer. Inscription on front of base 'The first of the few'. The jug stands 11¾" high (*see colour picture on page 104*). One sold at Phillips in Bath 1989 for **£1400/$2100**.

A John Peel Toby Jug was made with his date of birth 1776 and death 1854 around the base. In his hands he holds a fox's head and brush (tail), over his left shoulder is a hunting horn and the handle of jug is in the form of hunting whip. The jug stands 14½" high, c1915.

Six Toby Jugs were made marked: Newport Pottery Co.

10½" high raised no 859	6" high raised no 860	2½" high raised no 869
8" high raised no 862 m/s	4" high raised no	2¼" high raised no

Wilkinson bought out the Newport Pottery Co in 1925. It is interesting to note that Clarice Cliff joined Wilkinsons in 1916. The first Carruthers Gould jug 'Lord Kitchener' had only just been designed in 1915. Clarice Cliff's forte was pattern designing and not modelling. There is some doubt if she really did model or design any of these Tobies. In particular the John Peel, R.J. Mitchell, Chamberlain and Churchill jugs. It is a known fact that after 1939 some pottery shapes and designs were not hers, but were marked Clarice Cliff. See under Fakes.

Wood Family Jugs (Wood and Sons)

Colour picture on page 106.

Wood and Sons of Burslem closed their doors for the last time in December 1981 after 200 years of potting. During their last five years of existence they made six Toby Jugs, based on the 'original' jugs made in the eighteenth century. By careful photography of 'original' jugs, they were able to reproduce, in new moulds, faithful representations. The potting is a little on the thick side, but other than that the reproduction is very good and the jugs are becoming collectors' items in their own right. Because these jugs were produced in a limited edition, the moulds were destroyed after the required number had been produced, much to the regret of the makers – something that cannot be said of many so called 'limited editions' by other potters.

These limited edition reproduction Tobies are however considered to be among the best Toby Jugs made this century. Made in 1973. They are: 1000 Ordinary Toby Fillpot (with hat crown) modelled by Ernest Sambrooks; 1000 Martha Gunn modelled by Wilf Blandford; 1500 Benjamin Toby (raised glass) modelled by Wilf Blandford; 500 The Squire modelled by Wilf Blandford; 500 Admiral Lord Howe modelled by Wilf Blandford; 500 The Sailor modelled by Wilf Blandford; (The last four were made between 1975 and 1981)

Most of these jugs appear to have gone to the United States with the exception of the first two. I have in my collection the only all white 'Earl Howe' made to test the glaze.

Wood and Sons also produced twelve Dickens Toby Jugs for Franklin Mint c1978-81. These jugs were designed by Peter Jackson, the historical cartoonist.

Franklin Porcelain

In 1980 Franklin Porcelain commissioned Peter Jackson to design a set of twelve Tobies entitled 'The Cries of old London'. I'm not sure who did the modelling, but they were potted at Woods. They stand approximately 6¾" high and were issued during 1980 to 31st December 1980 in a limited edition world wide, over that period of time, at a cost of £30 each.

They were as follows:

The Coalman	The Chimney Sweep	The Old Clothes Man	The Door Mat Maker
The Flower Girl Vendor	The Orange Girl	The Milk Maid	The Baked Potato
The Street Doctor	The Oyster Woman	The Organ Grinder	The Umbrella Man

Tony Wood, the last member of the Wood family to be actively engaged in the industry, is a descendant of the famous Wood family of Burslem (eighth generation).

The 'Hearty Good Fellow' was made by Tony Wood (Studio 82) Ltd at Fenton, Stoke-on-Trent. This new company was formed by Tony Wood and Elizabeth Capper with the sole objective of continuing the fine tradition of design and manufacture carried out by the Wood family over the past 200 years. When at the factory in June 1983 I saw 'The Hearty Good Fellow' slightly smaller than the usual model, but I don't think it went into production as I have never seen another although Wilf Blandford, the modeller of this jug, tells me he has one. They were manufacturing a wide range of low priced Toby Jugs including small versions of 'Martha Gunn', the 'Sailor' and 'Earl Howe'.

In 1984 there was a fire at the Fenton factory, which resulted in Tony Wood going out of business, but the company has restarted under the management of Mark Bolton, under the name of Woods Pottery of Burslem, hence keeping the Woods name alive in the Staffordshire Potteries. One of the jugs which they will produce is the aforementioned 'Hearty Good Fellow'.

Royal Worcester

Colour picture on page 103.

This factory produced a small range of coloured Toby Jugs in the 1920s. Those jugs known are listed below, although there are believed to be others.

Punch and Judy	2"	1920s	Mephistopheles	7"	1927
Ordinary with cover	6"	1927			
Ordinary without cover	6"	1927	Ordinary with cover	3½"	1927

A small pair of Toby salt and pepper pots were also made in this period.

The value of these particular jugs is related to the desirability of Royal Worcester rather than their appeal as Toby Jugs. They are quite rare and prices have been recorded from **£75-£150/$105-$225.**

CHAPTER ELEVEN

Kevin Francis Ceramics

Prestige jugs designed and modelled by Peggy Davies
Kevin Francis have produced an enormous range of high quality Tobies in only a few short years. The first was of me! Peggy Davies was commissioned to model it and did such a fantastic job (though I say so myself), that they decided to produce others.

There is little doubt that these jugs are the finest detailed enamelled Tobies made this century. After studying at Burslem College of Art, Peggy Davies went to work for the Newport Pottery Company in Burslem as an assistant to Clarice Cliff. In 1939 she moved to Doulton in Burslem modelling many of their finest figurines until she started on her own, producing outstanding pieces of ceramic art. She worked with her son and four other assistants in her small pot bank situated amidst spectacular scenery in North Staffordshire on the Derbyshire border. One would be hard pressed to find pieces made by her bettered in the potteries today. Truly a name to go down in ceramic history. Sadly she died in June 1989.

The following are her first attempts at modelling a Toby Jug: Vic Schuler (the Toby collector) limited edition 1000 made 1988; Vic Schuler (the little Vic) limited edition 1500 made 1989; Sir Winston Churchill limited edition made 1988; The Shareholder limited edition 1500 made 1988; The Gardener limited edition 1500 made 1988; The Doctor limited edition 500 made 1988; The Postman limited edition made 1988

After Peggy Davies died in June 1989 three new artists were commissioned to design and model the Kevin Francis Toby Jugs: Douglas V. Tootle, who had worked for Wood & Sons, also Doultons; Geoff Blower, who also had worked for Doultons and Wedgwood; Andrew Moss, who had been apprenticed to Peggy Davies. Peggy's son Rod has always been in charge of the potting on all of these jugs and continues to do so at Peggy Davies Studio at Burslem.

Vic Schuler Toby 8¾" high

Colour picture on page 115
This was the first Toby Jug modelled by Peggy Davies. 1000 copies were made between February 1988 and February 1989. 650 had blue coats and 350 yellow, some twenty were made with the signatures of Peggy Davies and Vic Schuler impressed in the base. These were done to a special order on 7 November 1988 and came within the original 1000. There were some ten jugs made as a trial in various colours to ascertain which would be the best colours to use. One was glazed in all white and one left in the unglazed biscuit (which is now in the author's possession). Probably no two jugs are quite identical, as shades slightly vary, they were all hand painted and took approximately six hours each.

The unusual feature of the jug was that the cover of my first book *British Toby Jugs* was printed on the book held in the right hand and the Toby Jug in the left. This being a feature used for the first time since 'The Yorkshire Toby' of c1800. The initial cost of the jug was £90/$135 retail, but is now (1999) fetching **£400-£450/$720-$810**.

Frank, the '*Francis*' of Kevin Francis, was amazed at his first sight of the toby jug of myself. The design was superb and the quality of the potting second to none. His experience had taught him that this was a rare thing, and after initial scepticism was pleased that Kevin had made the first approaches to Rod and Peggy Davies. Frank felt that the ideas for the Doctor and the Cook etc that followed were a little weak, not because of the modelling, but because of the concept. He set about introducing famous characters like Winston Churchill and Clarice Cliff – which was to lead to the Artists and Potters series, and these were among their best selling themes. It seemed that Frank and Kevin were an excellent team together, each complimenting the other – Kevin initiating ideas and Frank rationalising them and putting them into practice. As time progressed, Frank became more and more involved in the ceramics side of the business, instigating a line of figurines and introducing Kevin Francis to a wider audience. Meanwhile Kevin turned to America for an attempt to expand the market. By the early 90s, Lawson's disastrous budgets of previous years had caused inflation and then recession in the UK. With Kevin in Chicago, now largely dealing in David Winter, it was left to Frank to find a way out of severe problems for the company. It had simply grown too quickly and could not withstand the rigours of a recession. Bravely, in 1994, he negotiated the company out of the quagmire. The partnership was to be dissolved and the company divided into three, Kevin keeping the US business he had developed, Rod taking control of the Kevin Francis business, and Frank himself developing the neglected publishing business. Since publishing had been Frank's initial inspiration, and the ceramics business Kevin's, it seemed that things had turned full circle. Rod's hard work and ability to produce top quality earned him the right to take on the precarious task of steering Kevin Francis to success. And it was extremely difficult for all of them. Kevin had to live for a while in his shop, Frank had to sell off most of his assets and build a publishing business from virtually nothing, and Rod had now to take on the financial burden of developing Kevin Francis during a heavy recession. But it worked. The ingredients that had made Kevin Francis such a storming success in the early years were still in place, and there can be no regrets. Rod Davies is now in charge of one of the best collectables in the UK – a real success story for all concerned. And just think – if it wasn't for Vic Schuler, Kevin Francis toby jugs would never even have been made in the first place!

Little Vic

Colour picture on page 114.
A small Ordinary type Toby Jug 6" high in the likeness of Vic Schuler. Held in the left hand is a foaming jug of ale and in the right a clay pipe, on the handle is a devil. The jug was modelled by Peggy Davies and was in fact the last work she did before her death in 1989. The jug was produced in two colours, one with a blue coat and black hat, the other with a white coat and hat. Made in a limited edition of 2500. Original retail price was £40/$60, but is now (1999) fetching £100/$200.

The following pages gives the complete listing of the Toby jugs produced by Kevin Francis.

Toby Jug		Year of introduction	Edition size	Market value	Colour pic page
Admiral Churchill (Blue) Admiral Churchill (White)	}	1992	750	£131/$235	109
American Sailor		1998	250	£165/$300	115
Douglas Bader		1990	750	£225-£275/$405-$540	109
Hannah Barlow		1991	350	£375-£425/$675-$765	109
Britannia		1993	350	£116/$210	109
Bugs Bunny (Warner Bros Commission)		1993	750	£250-£275/$450-$495	114
Bulldog Dinnertime		1992	150?	£300-£350/$540-$630	
Churchill (Boer)		1999	500	£155/$280	109
Churchill (D-Day)		1994	750	£147/$265	109
Churchill (Politician)		1993	750	£137/$245	
Churchill (VE Day)		1995	750	£147/$265	109
Churchill (Naval)		1994	650	£130/$235	109
Winston Churchill (Seated) (Black) Winston Churchill (Seated) (White) Winston Churchill (Seated) (Blue)	}	1989 1989 1991	5000	£147/$260	
Winston Churchill (Seated) (Mini)		1991	2500	£26/$45	
Churchill Standing (Blue) Churchill Standing (Black)	}	1990	750	£275-£300/$495-$540	109
Churchill Standing (mini)		1993	2500	£26/$45	
Clarice Cliff		1990	350	£500-£600/$900-$1080	110
Clarice Cliff (mini)		1993	2500	£26/$45	
Clown (Red) Clown (White) Clown (Black)	}	1989	1500	£275-£300/$495-$540	110
Columbus		1992	750	£115/$210	110
The Cook		1989	250	£225-£275/$405-$495	110
Susie Cooper		1991	350	£250-£350/$450-$630	110
Tommy Cooper		1997	Guild†	£119/$215	110
Daffy Duck (Warner Bros Commission)		1993	750	£250-£275/$450-$495	114
Salvador Dali		1992	350	£131/$235	110
Peggy Davies		1993	500	£147/$265	110

Doctor (Green) Doctor (Blue) }	1989	500	£250-£275 / $450-$495	110
Sir Henry Doulton	1992	350	£137 / $245	111
Drunken Sal (Classics)	1997	100*	£300-£375 / $540-$675	111
Duke of Wellington	1992	750	£121 / $215	113
General Eisenhower	1992	750	£121 / $215	
Fisherman (Blue) Fisherman (Green) }	1990	500	£225-£275 / $405-$495	111
The Gardener (Red) The Gardener (Yellow) }	1989	1500	£250-£275 / $450-$495	111
Golfer (Blue) Golfer (Brown) }	1990	1000	£225-£250 / $405-$450	111
Gin Woman	1999	100	£175 / $315	
President Gorbechov	1990	750	£131 / $235	111
President Gorbechov (mini)	1992	2500	£58 / $105	
Martha Gunn (Classics)	1996	100*	£345-£395 / $620-$710	111
Hearty Good Fellow (Blue) Hearty Good Fellow (Green) }	1990	750	£95 / $175	111
Sherlock Holmes	1992	750	£137 / $245	111
Henry VIII	1991	750	£137 / $245	112
Stonewall Jackson	1993	750	£121 / $215	111
John F Kennedy	1992	750	£225-£250 / $405-$450	112
Kings Dilemma (Edward VIII)	1997	350	£200-£250 / $360-$450	110
Kings of Comedy (Laurel & Hardy)	1994	Guild†	£119 / $215	112
Helmut Kohl	1991	999	£131 / $235	112
Sandra Kuck	1992	600	£137 / $245	112
Bernard Leach	1992	200	£250-£300 / $450-$555	113
Little Clarice	1991	2500	£58 / $110	
Little Golfer	1991	2500	£58 / $110	
Little Vic (Blue) Little Vic (White) }	1989	2500	£58 / $105	114
Little Winston (Black) Little Winston (Blue) }	1991	2500	£58 / $110	
Nelson Mandela	1995	250	£130 / $235	113
Marx Brothers	1995	Guild†	£119 / $215	112
Midshipmite – (John Major)	1993	750	£116 / $210	113
Max Miller	1999	Guild†	£119 / $215	113
Miniature Teddy (Brown) Miniature Teddy (White) }	1991	2500	£26 / $45	117
Montgomery (khaki) Montgomery (faded) }	1990	750	£121 / $220	113
William Moorcroft	1991	350	£375-£450 / $675-$810	111
Morecambe & Wise	1996	Guild†	£119 / $215	112
Captain Henry Morgan	1994	250	£131 / $235	113
Napoleon	1992	750	£121 / $215	113
General Patton	1991	750	£121 / $215	113
Pavarotti Sitting (Grey) Pavarotti Sitting (Black) }	1990	2000	£400 / $720	114
Pavarotti (Standing)	1990	250	£300-£400 / $540-$720	114
Pepe le Phew (Warner Bros Commission)	1993	750	£250-£275 / $450-$495	114
Pershore Miller	1991	1500	£200-£250 / $360-$450	114

Picasso	1992	350	£131/$235	114
Pope John Paul	1993	350	£150-£200/$270-$360	113
The Postman	1989	1500	£225-£250/$405-$450	114
Prince of Clowns	1993	Guild†	£119/$215	112
Elvis Presley	1993	Prototypes only £400/$800+		114
Princess Diana	1992	900	£116/$210	115
Queen Elizabeth II	1992	400	£131/$235	115
Queen Mother (Violet) Queen Mother (Rose)	1990	900	£131/$235	115
Charlotte Rhead	1991	350	£300-£375/$540-$675	115
Lucie Rie	1994	200	£175-£225/$315-$405	115
Rocking Santa	1995	2500	£30/$50	115
Rommell	1991	750	£121/$215	115
Henry Sandon	1995	750	£105/$190	116
Santa Claus	1989	1500	£225-£275/$405-$495	
Vic Schuler (Blue) Vic Schuler (Yellow)	1988	1000	£400-£450/$720-$810	115
Shakespeare (Dark Blue) Shakespeare (Light Blue)	1990	1000	£131/$235	116
The Shareholder (Green) The Shareholder (Blue)	1989	1500	£250-£275/$495-$540	116
Snuff Taker (Classics)	1998	100*	£300-£375/$540-$675	116
The Squire	1993	750	£131/$235	116
Stormin Norman	1991	750	£121	116
Sylvester (Warner Bros Commission)	1993	750	£250-£275/$450-$495	114
Tasmanian Devil (Warner Bros Commission)	1993	750	£250-£275/$450-$495	114
Margaret Thatcher (Blue) Margaret Thatcher (Polka)	1989	1000	£131/$235	116
Margaret Thatcher (Spitting Image)	1991	650	£61/$110	
Thin Man (Green) Thin Man (Pink)	1997	250	£165/$300	117
George Tinworth	1993	350	£137/$245	116
Toby Fillpot	1992	750	£131/$235	117
Dick Turpin	1995	250	£131/$235	117
Van Gogh	1993	350	£131/$235	117
Joshia Wedgwood	1991	350	£137/$245	117
Moe Wideman	1992	350	£137/$245	117
David Winter	1991	950	£300-£350/$540-$630	117
Ralph Wood	1992	350	£131/$235	117
Ralph Wood (mini)	1993	Guild†	£50-£60/$90-$110	
Boris Yeltsin	1991	250	£137/$245	117

* Classic Collection pieces were a limited edition of 100 pieces painted to individual customers requirements
† Guild Exclusives edition size is limited to the number of Guild members who ordered

Kevin Francis has always produced limited editions, and because of the high standard set by Peggy Davies before her death, this has continued. As you can see, once out of production, many of these models fetch a premium on the secondary market – making them highly collectable. Many of these listed here will be out of production soon.

Victorian

Toby teapot holding spout, c1850, £80.

In Saltglaze brown, Stone ware King George III, c1850, £400.

George III in White Porcelain and lined in gold. Date and Maker unknown. £300+.

Cross Legged Toby with pipe on lap c.1850.

Cross Legged Toby with Willow Pattern coat and hat with raised letters on base £200 'Sampson Smith 1851 Longton'.

Snuff Taker toby teapot with orange lustre coat. c1860. £200.

Merry Christmas probably by Sampson Smith 1860, £200

'The Landlord' 'Home Brewed Ale by Sampson Smith 1860 £250

Man in Barrel, c1864, by White & Ridge, £300.

Snuff Taker c1870, in Meashamware. On front printed "Good Health Ol' chap'. £300.

Mr Pickwick, c1875.

Falstaff in polychromatic colours, 1880 £200

Ten tobies, the tallest 1¾", Punch by Denton, small. £15 each.

From left: two 1½" females, £15 each; centre: 2¾" Devonmoor, £20; right: two 1¾" by Stephen Hancock, Derby, small, £80 each.

Five Squat Tobies, under £100 each. Bottom left and right Copeland Spode

Six Snuff Takers, tallest 6", c1850. £40 each.

Tumbler toby, inscribed 'Fulham 1864-1889', £200.

Barrister late 19th century £500

The Landlord, late 19th century, £200.

Four Snuff Takers, c1850, tallest 6" £40 each.

Male and Female Tobies in majolica ware by Sharpe Brothers & Co, c1880, £80 each.

20th Century

Hunch Back Toby, c1900, £50.

Hands in Pockets Toby, Methven. Links Pottery, Kirkcaldy, c1900(?), £100.

Ordinary with fake date, c1900, £50.

John Bull by William Kent, c1900, £70.

Snuff Taker by Allerton, £50.

Barrister. Minton, 1903, £300.

Nelson by William Kent, 1903, £50.

'I'm on the Black List', incised "Made in England, Rd No. 476210" (1906) £70.

'Black Man' Incised Branham, 1910, £200

Old Bill, c1917, £200.

Two by William Ault, left: Peace made in 1919, £250 and right: Titbits from 1917, £100.

*Charlie Chaplin by Doulton,
1918, £2000.*

Doulton Double XX Tobies, stoneware by Harry Simeon, c1910-20.

Doulton by Harry Simeon, 1910-20, $2^1/_2$" to $8^1/_2$".

*Fiddler by Frank Stoner
1920 £600.*

The Motorist, c1920

Above: Characterture of Sir F. Carruthers Gould, printed in Vanity Fair, 22 February, 1890.

A group of famous people Tobies, The Botha and the Churchill are very rare at £1500 each. The remainder are worth about £400 each.

Two Admiral Jellicoe Tobies, designed by Sir F. Carruthers-Gould. Left, the standard model, £300; right: rare model only one recorded, £1000+.

Punch, by William Kent, early to mid 20th century £80.

Ordinary, c1920 made by Shorter & Sons, 12½", £80.

Doulton Huntsmen by Harry Fenton, c1920.

George Robey, Doulton, 1926, £3000

Above: Three Squires, from left: Wood & Sons, c1980, £200; William Kent(?), c1920, £300; W. Kent, c1920, £200.

Right: Tobies by Devomoor, 1½" to 23¼" high.

Four Squires, from left £700; £1200; William Kent, c1920 £200; William Kent, c1960, £100.

Winston Churchill by W. H. Goss, 1927, £200.

Lloyd George, c1930, maker unknown, 7". £200.

Five Tobies by Clarice Cliff, Newport Pottery, £500.

Tobies made by an unknown maker, c1930 from left: Ramsay McDonald; Stanley Baldwin; Sir Harry Lauder. £200 each.

From left: Beefeater, Burleigh & Co £100; Tax Man, Wedgwood & Co, £100; and Lord Mayor, Wedgwood & Co, £100.

Tobies by Royal Worcester produced between c1929 and 1933. Sizes range between $1^3/_4$", $3^1/_2$" and $5^3/_4$" (£500+).

Elihu Yale, Wedgwood, 1933.

Reginald J. Mitchell by Wilkinson, c1940, £1500.

President F. D. Roosevelt by Copeland Spode, c1945.

'Fiddler' by Beswick 1948 £100.

Centre two: 2¹/₂" high Paragon (£200). The outer four, Doulton, (£400).

Left: Winston Churchill made by Burgess & Leigh, 1941. (£150).

A 1948 reproduction of Mr Gladstone, which has printed on base:
Sampson Smith
Est 1846
Olde Staffordshire Figures
from Original Moulds
No 3 Mr Gladstone

Mikado characters made by Shorter and Son, c1949, 9³/₄" high, from left: Pooh-Ba, Ko-Ko and Mikado. £400 each.

Back, Sir Winston Churchill made by from left: Clarice Cliff, Kirkland, Copland Spode and two by Burleigh; Front: four from Doulton, Leonard Jarvis and finally Brannam.

Winston Churchill by Leonard Jarvis, £1600.

Lord Mackintosh by Leonard Jarvis, £2000.

Left: Shylock 9"; and right The Teller, 8¹/₂" both Wain (Melba ware), 1950s, £100.

Earl Howe, in a White Glaze. Wood and Sons 1975 £200.

Rev Tubby Clayton without spectacles, the only one made.

Rev Tubby Clayton, made by Ken Speaks.

Two examples from Wedgwood & Co, left: Coachman; and Nightwatchman c1895.

Two unknown 20th century potters produced these, left, thought to be made in West Grinstead, Sussex and right incised on back 'Rickwood', probably by an amateur.

Left: Tobies produced by Wood & Sons between 1973 and 1981 (£150 each).

Abraham Lincoln by Staffordshire Fine Ceramics, c1980, £1000.

Top left: Beadle, Friar Tuck, and Town Crier; Bottom: Poor Man, Sweep, made by Roy Kirkham, 1981.

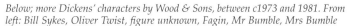

Dickens figures from Wood & Sons, from left: Jacob Marley, Artful Dodger, Sairy Gamp, figure not known and Scrooge.

Below; more Dickens' characters by Wood & Sons, between c1973 and 1981. From left: Bill Sykes, Oliver Twist, figure unknown, Fagin, Mr Bumble, Mrs Bumble

Goss c1930, £150

Goss, £100.

Sleeping Toby by Cliff Adkins. £100.

The largest Toby in the world to date at 39" made by Old Algreave Pottery, Left fully painted and right as it comes out of the mould.

Kevin Francis

Douglas Bader, 1990, £225-£275/$405-$540.

Hannah Barlow, 1991, £375-£425/$675-$765.

Britannia, 1993, £116/$210.

Admiral Churchill, 1992, £131/$235.

Winston Churchill (VE), 1995, £147/$265

Winston Churchill (D-Day), 1994, £147/$265.

Winston Churchill in black and blue colourways, 1990, £275-£300/$495-$540.

Naval Winston Churchill, 1994, £130/$235.

Boer Churchill, 1999, £155/$280.

Clarice Cliff, 1990, £500-£600/$900-$1080.

Clown, 1989, £275-£300/$495-$540.

Columbus, 1992, £115/$210.

The Cook, modelled by Peggy Davies, 1989, £225-£275/ $405-$495.

Susie Cooper, 1991, £250-£350/$450-$630.

Tommy Cooper, 1997, Guild piece, £119/$215.

Salvador Dali, 1992, £131/ $235.

Peggy Davies, 1993, £147/ $265.

The Doctor, modelled by Peggy Davies , 1989, £250-£275/$450-$495.

The Kings Dilemma, (Edward VIII and Mrs Simpson), 1997, £200-£250/ $360-$450.

Two characters from the history of ceramics, left: Sir Henry Doulton, 1992, £137/$245; and right, William Moorcroft, 1991, £375-£450/$675-$810.

Drunken Sal, 1997, £300-£375/$540-$675.

The Fisherman, 1990, £225-£275/$405-$495.

The Gardener, modelled by Peggy Davies, 1989, £250-£275/$450-$495.

The Golfer, modelled by Andy Moss, 1990, £225-£250/ $405-$450.

President Gorbechov, modelled by Andy Moss, 1990, £131/$235.

Martha Gunn, 1996, £345-£395/$620-$710.

Hearty Good Fellow (Vic Schuler), 1990, £95/$175.

Sherlock Holmes, 1992, £137/$245

Stonewall Jackson, 1993, £121/$215.

Henry VIII, 1991, £137/ $245.

John F Kennedy, 1992,Left the model that went into production, £225-£250/$405-$450; right shows a prototype

Helmut Kohl, 1991, £131/ $235

Sandra Kuck, 1992, £137/ $245.

Prince of Clowns (Charlie Chaplin), 1993, £119/$215; Kings of Comedy (Oliver Hardy with Stan Laurel handle), 1994, £119/$215; Eric Morecambe (Ernie Wise handle), 1996, £119/$215; Groucho Marx (Harpo and Chico handle), 1995, £119/$215.

Bernard Leach, 1992, £250-£300/$450-$555.

Nelson Mandela, 1995, £130/$235

Three 20th Century Fiddler Jugs. Left Beswick, Centre John Major by Kevin Francis, 1993, £116/$210. Right by Frank Stoner.

Max Miller, 1999, £119/$215.

Captain Henry Morgan, 1994, £131/$235.

Napoleon and Wellington, 1992, £121/$215 each.

General Patton, 1991, £121/$215.

Pope John Paul, 1993, £150-£200/$270-$360.

General Montgomery, 1990, £121/$220.

Another version of Luciano Pavarotti, 1990, £400/$720.

Luciano Pavarotti, 1990, £300-£400/$585-$720.

Pershone Miller, 1991, £200-£250/$360-$450.

Picasso, 1992, £131/$235.

Cartoon characters from the Looney Tunes Series commissioned by Warner Brothers, from left: Pepe le Phew, Bugs Bunny, Daffy Duck, Tasmanian Devil and Sylvester, £250-£275/$450-$495 each.

Elvis Presley, 1993, prototype (only six made).

Postman, 1989, £225-£250/ $405-$450.

'Little Vic' (Vic Schuler), 1989, £58/$105.

Princess Diana, 1992, £116/ $210.

Princess Diana, prototype.

Queen Elizabeth the Queen Mother, 1990, £131/$235

Queen Elizabeth II, 1992, £131/$235.

Charlotte Rhead, 1991, £300-£375/$540-$675.

Lucie Rie, 1994, £175-£225/$315-$405.

Rommel, 1991, £121/$215.

American Sailor, 1998, £165/ $300.

Above and right: Vic Schuler by Peggy Davies, 1988, £400-£450/$720-$810.

Rocking Santa, 1995, £30/$50.

115

Henry Sandon, 1995, £105/ $190.

Gen. Norman Schwartzkopf. Available worldwide except US where it was withdrawn after complaint, 1991, £121.

William Shakespeare, 1990, £131/$235.

The Shareholder, modelled by Peggy Davies, 1989, £250-£275/$495-$540.

Snuff-Taker, 1998, £300-£375/$540-$675

Margaret Thatcher, 1989, £131/$235.

The Squire, 1993, £131/ $235.

George Tinworth, 1993, £137/$245.

Thin Man, 1997, £165/$300.

Toby Fillpot, 1992, £131/ $235.

Dick Turpin, 1995, £131/ $235.

Van Gogh, 1993, £131/$235.

Josiah Wedgwood, 1991, £137/$245.

Moe Wideman, 1992, £137/ $245.

David Winter, 1991, £300-£350/$540-$630.

Ralph Wood, 1992, £131/ $235.

Boris Yeltsin, 1991, £137/ $245, surrounded by Miniature Teddy, 1991, £26/$45.

Advertising and other types of toby

Burkes Whiskey, c1890 by S. Fielding & Co..

Left: Johnnie Walker 14½", made by Ashtead c1925. Right: John Peel 14½", made by Wilkinson c1915.

The Toby Convertible Chair Co, c1930, £100/$170.

Hoare, c1933.

Toby Ale, from left: Doulton, Wood & Sons, and a Fielding & Co with a musical movement.

RSM Tibby Brittain by Melwood, c1976, for Bell's Whiskey.

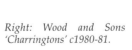

Arnold Elliott by Melwood c1978.

Right: Wood and Sons 'Charringtons' c1980-81.

'Bass' Lord Mayor by Beswick, 1985.

Miscellaneous

The Town Crier, gold anchor mark, Sitsendorf, Germany, £100/$170.

Six tobies the tallest 3³/₄", three in pottery, one stoneware, one porcelain, one Sheford plate, small, £50/$85 each.

Toby cup and saucer, Burlington ware, £30/$51.

Toby used as a funeral urn. Size is about 8¾" and bears the inscription 'Catherine Hawkins' on the base.

Small jug Sheffield plate 19th Century. Large jug, pewter by Turtin of Sheffield, c1920.

Toby moneybox, early 19th century, £200/$340; Smokers Companion, probably by Devonmoor, c1930.

Toby in black basalt by Roy Kirkham, c1973 4¾".

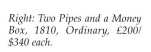

Right: Two Pipes and a Money Box, 1810, Ordinary, £200/$340 each.

Five Standing Tobies, 4½", 19th century, £50/$85 each.

Five Standing Tobies, 4½", 19th century, £50/$85 each.

Six Standing Tobies, 4½", 19th century, £50/$85 each.

Five Standing Tobies, 4½", 19th century, £50/$85 each

Blue and White Condiments Set of 4. Mid 19th Century. £400/$680.

Willow Pattern Condiments Set Mid 19th Century, £600/$1020.

Condiments Set 1850 £50/$85 each.

Various Condiments 1850 £50/$85 each

Four tobies sitting on floor, 3", 19th century, £50/$85 each.

Sir Winston Churchill

There are seventeen Tobies of Churchill at least. The first was by W. H. Goss in 1927. It stands 6½" high in both blue and green coats and shows him sitting on a chair with his hands in a praying position. Printed on his top hat is the phrase: 'Any odds — bar one, that's me who kiss the Blarney Stone'. *See picture on page 102.*

Doulton

Colour picture on page 105.
Designer H. Fenton. Made in three sizes. Stands 4", 5½", 9" high. 1941. Showing Churchill seated. This jug was still in Doultons catalogue in 1990.

Burgess & Leigh

Colour picture on page 104.
Designed by E.T. Bailey. (Two jugs made) Churchill as John Bull (standing) 1941, Churchill making 'V' sign (seated) 1941. **Value £100/$150+**

Copeland Spode

Designer Eric Olsen. Churchill smoking cigar. 8½" high. Issued in bright blue and yellow enamels. Also in all over white 1945-1952 as it is thought no coloured ware was permitted in Britain at this time. Designed in 1941.

Kirkland (Etruria)

Colour picture on page 105.
Seated with detachable top hat 1941.

Beswick

Designed by Mr Watkins. 7" high model no 931 1941, withdrawn 1954. With detachable top of head and hat. **Value: £200/$300.**

W. Brannam of Barnstaple, Devon

Colour picture on page 105.
In old style dress with top hat. Various colours issued 1941.

Lancaster

Designed by Sandland. Seated figure with lion rampant handle c1941.

Wilkinsons Ltd

Designed by Clarice Cliff (Royal Staffordshire Pottery Co of Burslem) 1941, 12" high. Showing Churchill dressed in the uniform of Lord Warden of the Cinque Ports. Holding in his hands a battleship. He is sitting on a bull dog which is draped with the union flag. Around the base is inscribed 'Going into action, may God defend the right'.

Floral China

Churchill dressed in naval uniform, seated 1941.

Leonard Jarvis

Colour picture on page 105.

Without doubt this is one of the finest twentieth century Toby Jugs that has been made. Sir Winston Churchill was modelled by Leonard Jarvis and possesses the fine translucent glazes of the R. Wood type. Its conception was inspired by Lord Mackintosh and it shows Churchill in his famous 'Victory' pose with the two fingers of his right hand raised. His left hand holds a palette and brushes and at his foot is a pile of letters with an ink well and quill pen on top, whilst there is a trowel at his left foot. We thus see Winston Churchill for his many attributes, as war leader, painter, brick layer and writer. Some were painted with a blue/green coat and hat, others yellow. Made some date before 1968. One sold at Bute sale in July 1996 for **£1840/$3680** with buyers premium.

Staffordshire Fine Ceramics

Seated Toby with No. 10 on seat. Limited edition of 1000. Issued 1987. **Value: c£100/$150.**

Kevin Francis Ceramics

Colour picture on page 109.

1989   Modelled by Peggy Davies. Limited edition 5000. Seated with lion at his left leg. Holding cigar in his right hand. At his right side is his book 'The History of the English Speaking Peoples'. The handle is in the form of the Union flag. The jug stands 8¾" high, around the base is printed in Latin 'The nation had the lions heart. I provided the roar.' The jug comes in two colours, black coat and hat with striped trousers and with white coat, hat and trousers.

1990   A standing Churchill with a 'V' shaped handle. 9" high.

1991   5" Churchill with Bulldog astride British Isles. Modelled by Douglas V. Tootle.

1992   9" Naval Churchill. Modelled by Douglas V. Tootle.

1993   9" Political Churchill with Bulldog. Modelled by Douglas V. Tootle.

1995   9" Churchill 50th Anniversary V.E. Day.

1999   Churchill in Boer War uniform

CHAPTER THIRTEEN

White, Salt Glaze, Measham and Lustre Tobies

All White Toby

An all-white or cream Toby jug may not sound very attractive, but when standing on a shelf of polychrome Tobies, these jugs look most impressive, especially if the jug is lightly potted with crisp, fine detail. The same can be said for brown stoneware, and they make a nice contrast when placed side by side.

Ralph Wood and Neal & Co. seem to have made all-white Toby Jugs along with other potters in the eighteenth century. As a result of their plainness these jugs never seem to reach the higher prices of their polychrome brothers.

Brown Salt Glaze Stoneware Tobies

It would seem that no Toby Jugs were made in this ware before c1824; but once in production they were made in potteries all over Britain. Derbyshire was one area where they were produced, by potteries such as: S & H Briddon and Matthew Knowles & Son of Brampton; J Oldfield & Co, near Chesterfield; and J. Bourne and Son of Denby.

They were also potted by potteries in London, in the Lambeth and Fulham districts. See under 'Tumbler Toby' John Carrol.

Snuff-takers are also common in this ware, see under 'The Snuff Taker'. A third figure shows Toby sitting on a barrel lying on its side. This Jug is about 6" high and can be seen in the Victoria and Albert Museum but as it does not have a handle, so it cannot really be classed as a Toby Jug.

The glory of most of these brown salt glaze jugs is that what they lack in colour they make up for in crisp modelling detail.

In this ware I find the Tobies made by Oldfield and Co. the most interesting, with often a lustrous glaze, the mark

Oldfield & Co
Makers

is usually impressed between the legs of the chair on the back.
See colour picture on page 69.

All cream Toby (R. Wood?) c1790.

Salt glazed stoneware marked Brampton, (8½") c1825.

Rockingham Brown Treacle Glaze Tobies

See colour picture on page 80.
The Brameld family managed the Rockingham pottery which was situated on the Earl of Fitzwilliam's Estate near Swinton, Yorkshire. They produced a manganese brown, lead-glaze Toby and two examples of early Snuff Takers have been recorded as having the impressed 'Rockingham' mark on them. This type of pottery was made after 1826, when Rockingham first started producing this ware and although there are other producers, 'Rockingham' has become the generic term for this type of pottery.

These Tobies are particularly uninteresting in that they tend to lack detail, but the early ones do have a more attractive variation of colour tones. The later ones, made well into the twentieth century, are more uniform and dull. The Toby types in this ware are: the 'Standing Man' which appears to be the rarest, the Ordinary Toby, 'The Gin Woman', 'The Snuff Taker teapot', and most commonly, 'The Snuff Taker'.

Rockingham also made a pair of male and female Snuff Takers in all over cream colour with gilding, c1830. The man with hat crown is 8½" high and the woman 9". There is some doubt that these were made at Rockingham, some think Staffordshire, but they are always referred to as Rockingham. Value: £60/$90

Meashamware Bargeware

Colour picture on page 79.

Meashamware bargeware is unique in that it was made during a sixty to seventy year period between the 1850s/1860s and 1920s. It was made around the Swadlincote/Woodville area of South Derbyshire possibly on the site where the factory of Mason and Cash/Cloverleaf is currently situated. It was sold from a hut on the banks of the canal at Measham in Leicestershire, which was part of the Birmingham ring canal system; that stretch of the canal system was filled in during the 1930s. As far as we know the main potter was one man – Bossy Mason. Canal folk bought them for every day use off the shelf, but at least an equal quantity of specially commissioned pieces were made for the barge people who would order them for presents for friends and relations on their way to their delivery destination and pick them up on their return journey. This is why bargeware can be found all over the UK and not just in the Midlands area. Teapots were the most popular item made but other pottery included tea kettles and stands, jugs, mugs (called 'clouts'), goblets, sugar bowl and cream jug, tobacco jars, candlesticks and spittoons and even a chamber pot; the pieces were specially commissioned for presents often had the recipients' name included in the decoration and items were sometimes dated. Various different sizes were availale in teapots, from one pint to two gallons, including some two spouters. Most have a small teapot on the lid as a knob.

Meashamware Snuff Taker.

To find toby jugs in this ware is very rare. I know of only three, one of which I own, a Snufftaker, on his belly impressed in blue on a white cartouche is 'Good health old chap', and is 8¾" high. The other is owned by Judi Bland is a Gin Woman, impresed on her front is 'Drink up old dame', and one other Gin Woman has been recorded.

According to local people, they were also bought by hawkers who came on their donkeys and bought them by the cartload, taking them through the villages and sleeping 'rough' with the donkey. The gallon pots were sold for half a crown and the half-galloners for one shilling and sixpence!

Lustre Tobies

Colour picture on page 74.

Some Tobies from around the early part of the nineteenth century were made in 'lustre' which became quite popular; copper, gold and silver lustre being fairly common, pink lustre coats less so, making these Tobies something of a collector's item. Pink lustre is usually associated with Sunderland.

Jugs recorded in this medium are:

Cross legged All over gold lustre c1850.
King or Prince Hal All over silver lustre 15" high. On the small shield held in left hand are the initials G.R. (probably George IV). A very rare jug.
Yorkshire Ordinary All over silver lustre 9½" high with figure head handle. Rare jug.
Gin Woman All over copper lustre.
Snuff Taker All over silver lustre 9½" high. All over copper lustre.
Squat Toby These are found in both all over silver and copper lustre.
Nelson All over copper lustre 11¼" high.
Nelson Gold lustre epaulettes, hailing trumpet and sword guard. Silver lustre cannon. 11¼" high.
Standing Miniatures In silver lustre coat 4½" high.
Ordinary In pink lustre coat. These are rare, only four have been recorded.
Sitting Black Man There is a silvery pink lustre on the decoration on small jug held in hands.
Standing man All over silver lustre.
Coachman (large hands Toby) Holding silver lustre jug.
Man sitting in armchair All over copper lustre. Approx 6". Marked Roddy Ware Lustres. Staff. Eng.
Punch All over silver lustre, There is probably a 'Judy' to match (pair).
George Whitfield (Nightwatchman) All over silver lustre.
Snuff Taker Toby Teapot With orange lustre coat.
The value of all these would be around **£100-£200/$150-$300.**

There were sixteen pot banks in the Sunderland and Wearside area. To date, there appears to be no evidence of Toby Jugs being made in the Sunderland potteries, and neither are Toby Jug's mentioned in *Sunderland Pottery*, revised edition 1984 by John C Baker, BA AMA.

Pink Lusture was made in many areas other than Sunderland.

CHAPTER FOURTEEN

Toby Jugs other than in Pottery

Brass

The only brass Tobies that I have seen are a set of three in cast brass, quite well modelled, the sizes are 3", 4⅝", 5⅛". Probably made since 1960. **Not very valuable.**

Glass

The jugs found in this material are twentieth century much like a pint beer mug but cast in the form of a Toby. Using three moulds front and back and a handle. They are to be found in clear glass, also in pale green or blue about 6" high. Twentieth century made by 'Whitefriars Glass'. **Value: £30/$45.**

Three Brass Tobies c1970. £30/$51.

Leather

These always have the appearance of great antiquity but are probably no earlier than c1800. The one illustrated opposite was auctioned at Christies sale rooms, London in June 1987, but failed to reach its reserve price of £400/$600, as it was only bid to **£220/$330.** Height 10".

Pewter

These jugs must be quite rare, as I have been unable to find any information about them or locate anyone who has seen another. They stand 7" high, have a hinged lid (hat) and cain bound handle, the whole jug is very finely worked by any standards. On the bottom is stamped:

'Hall o' England' John Turtin Sheffield Pewter

In fact the metal is nearer to 'Britannia metal' than pewter, probably made in the first quarter of this century judging by its general style. **Value: £50-£100/$75-$150.**

Plaster

There are a number of Toby Jugs in plaster. All are of extremely poor quality, especially among the common sizes of 2" or 3" high. Probably one of the better quality items is the 9¼" high Ordinary with the raised glass in right hand, see under Charrington Tobies. **Value: £20/$30.**

Pewter c1920, made by Turtin of Sheffield, £50-£100/$75-$150.

Blue glass Toby by Whitefriars, £30/$45.

Leather c1800, £220/$330.

Porcelain

Most Tobies found made in porcelain are continental. Although many of the modern small twenieth century jugs, such as Crest Ware are in this material. Remember, pottery is opaque and porcelain is transparent, so the best method of testing is to hold the jug up to the light. Look through the top, and placing your fingers on the underside. If they can be seen, then the jug is porcelain.

Also a jug around 10" high will be quite heavy compared with a pottery jug of the same size.

Most of the Tobies found with the gold anchor mark at the back, or on the bottom of handle, are porcelain.

Rubber

Ordinary type standing 8" high. Handpainted c1930, the attached label reads: 'Castleware' made in England. Guaranted. Washable. Unbreakable. Waterproof. **Value: £30/$45**

Sheffield plate

The only ones I have encountered in this medium are the 3½" high standing miniature, made c1850, there is also an identical one in silver. **Value: £70/$105** – Silver **£150/$215**

Silver

There are probably a number of variations of Toby Jugs in silver. There are of course ⅜" high charm bracelet types. A very fine 'Hearty Good Fellow' was made in Germany c1870, standing approx. 11½" high and weighing 25 ozs, set with semi precious stones. In November 1993, R. Feldmans Ltd of The London Silver Vaults, had one priced at **£2000/$3000** and H. Perovetz Ltd at **£3850/$5775**. A 9" high Ordinary type Toby in silver with continental marks was sold at Christies, South Kensington, London on 5 September, 1989 for **£800/$1200**.

Terracotta

Which really is pottery defined by being a reddish, unglazed earthenware. The one illustrated on page 106 is probably unique. It was made, one would think by an amateur potter. The Toby figure is sitting holding a mug in his left hand and a bottle in the other, impressed on the base is the name 'Rickwood', the jug stands 9" high and quite crudely potted. These are not particularly valuable.

Tin

There is a 'Huntley & Palmer' biscuit tin made c1909 (Reg no. 569652) in the form of a Toby Jug, complete with hat, which acts as a hinged lid. The tin stands 6¼" high painted in enamel colours. Collected more by tin enthusiasts than Toby collectors. **Value: £100/$150.**

There is also a Mackintosh's Quality Street Toffee Tin, 5½" dia. This is not in Toby form, but has nine pictures of Toby Jugs depicted around the sides and on the lid. As one would expect from Lord Mackintosh one of the great collectors of Toby Jugs, they are all classic Tobies, probably from his own collection, 'Shield Toby', 'Sharp Face', 'Rodney Sailor', 'Thin Man', 'Raised Glass, Winston Churchill', 'Lord Howe', 'Prince Hal', 'The Squire'.

Wood

A rare and unusual early nineteenth century wooden Toby money box, 15" high, sold at R. H. Ellis & Sons auction rooms in Worthing, Sussex on 24 February, 1992. It represented an auctioneer holding a gavel in his right hand. The hammer price was **£2600/$3900**.

Another unique Toby, is hand carved in wood and bears the initials J.W. on the small jug. It is painted with a black hat complete with hat crown, brown jacket, yellow waistcoat and green breeches. The jug stands 13" high and was sold at Christies, King Street, London for **£300/$450** in February 1988.

A very fine carved Toby may be seen in Treen collection of Edward H. Pinto at the Birmingham Museum.

CHAPTER FIFTEEN

Advertising Tobies

Charrington Toby Jugs

Colour picture on page 118.
These jugs all have the characteristic of the right hand raised holding a glass up to the mouth. Otherwise one would refer to them as being an Ordinary Toby, 8¾" high. Usually wearing a green coat, red breeches, white stockings with black shoes and tricorn hat. They are found with different makers marks on the base:

Doulton. 1934, with the wording around base 'One Toby leads to another', or 'Toby ale' 'Toby' 'Toby ale'. These two by far are the best quality jugs.

Crown Devon. Fieldings made in England. 'Charrington Toby ale'.
This same jug was made with a musical movement in the base. Playing 'There is a tavern in the town' (made by Fielding) and again the same jug but with no inscription or makers marks but playing the same tune. But other tunes are known. This is almost identical to the Doulton Jug.

Wade. 7¼". 'Charrington beers' 'Charrington' 'Charrington beers'. Also made by Wade with only the printed word 'Charrington' on front, 6½" high.
The same jugs were made for Hoare and Company, a brewery which was bought out by Charringtons in 1934. These were potted by **James Green and Nephew Ltd**, London, designers and manufacturers. Around base is printed: 'Hoare & Company Toby Ale In Bottle'. Also the same but potted by The Associated Potteries, sole proprietors, **Hancock, Corfield and Walker**, Mitcham, London and The Potteries. Also marked Hancock & Corfield, Mitcham, London. **All the above are worth c£150/$225.**
Also a Toby made in Papier Mache with raised glass, around base is printed 'Charrington's, Toby Charrington's' and under the base in raised letters:

Beritex Hancor Mitcham

The same Toby but with no inscription was made by Lancaster, 'Sandland' Character Ware Hanley. This jug has a very chalky body. Also one was made in plaster but this is not a hollow jug. Probably made to stand on a pub bar, often has no markers name or inscription, but sometimes is printed on base 'Charringtons'.
Sandland also made the same raised glass Toby in glazed pottery, but is solid and quite heavy, probably filled with sand (no pun on the makers name intended), as its intended use was to stand on a pub bar counter as a match striker, the top being infilled with an abrasive surface such as sandpaper. c1950+
A plaster Toby only 3" high with 'Charringtons' on front was made, but maker unknown.

Wood & Sons. This company made a Toby c1980-81. 7¾" high with 'Charrington' imprinted on both sides of base in script lettering, 'Toby' on front in capital letters.
The coat is olive green, breechers red, hat and shoes, black and cream stockings. The jug appears to have been commissioned by Bass Charringtons of Burton-on-Trent.
An almost identical jug was made by Tony Wood, 7" high. The coat is red, breeches and shoes cream and stockings yellow, but this jug had no inscription around the base and is very common. It was still able to be purchased new in 1992.

Burkes Green Label Whiskey

S. Fielding & Co Ltd, Stoke on Trent
Colour picture on page 118.
This pottery started in 1879 and is still in business.
In the twentieth century marks used were:

S.F & Co England

accompanied with logo of a lion on a crown or with a crown imposed on a shield.
Also the trade name 'Crown Devon'.

A Toby which at first glance one would think was made in Holland or France, by the style of decoration, is very light, standing 11¼" high. It depicts a man sitting on a barrel holding a glass in his left hand and a bottle in the right. On the front of the barrel is written:

Burkes Green Label Whiskey.
The Whiskey of Individual Charm.
Exquisitely Mellow, Light and Digestive.

Showing a sitting cat and three stars. On the base is impressed 75 and in black underglaze Fieldings Stoke on Trent. This jug is quite rare, probably made c1890.

Bells Whiskey

Colour picture on page 118.

Melwood made two Tobies which concern this book. They are of Regimental Sergeant Major 'Tibby' Brittain of the Coldstream Guards 1918-1955, who trained 40000 officers and was said to have the loudest voice in the British Army. It was designed by Allen Sly and made in a limited edition of 300 for Arthur Bell Distillers in 1976. The figure is in the form of a 'Town Cryer', ringing a bell, which must be a pun on Bells Whiskey. The jug is 8" high, draped over the left leg is a scroll on which is the coat of arms of Bells Whiskey company.

The other jug is of Arnold Elliott the publican of 'The Bell' at Hillmorton near Rugby, Warwickshire. This jug was made in a limited edition of 500 to raise funds for The Licensed Victuallers National Homes c1978. The jug stands approx. 6" high.

Johnny Walker Whiskey

Colour picture on page 118.

A jug 15" high showing the traditional Johnny Walker figure sitting in red frock coat and grey top hat. Around the base is printed Killmarnock, still going strong Johnny Walker, born 1820, and on the underside:

Ashstead Potters
Percy Metcalfe
Rd No 720295
Made in England

Quite a rare jug, the only one seen by me had the limited edition no. 453 so one would assume that at least 500 were made in 1925. Stephen Mullin has one in his museum in Chicago.

The Toby Convertible Chair Co

Colour picture on page 118.

Made c1930. Ordinary Toby 6¼" high in majolica type glazes of blue, green and brown. Printed in black on the unglazed base:

With the compliments of
the 'Toby'
Convertible
Chair Co
2 Ludgate Hill
London, E.C.4.

Value £100/$10.

Cognac Martell Brandy

Made by Sandland, Hanley, Staff after 1952. This is not strictly a Toby jug as it only shows a figure waist high wearing a black coat and yellow waistcoat. He sports a monocle and in his right hand holds a brandy glass. Around the base is printed 'Cognac Martell Brandy'. The jug is 6½" high. **Value: £100/$150.**

Bass

Colour picture on page 118.

Made by Beswick, it depicts a standing Lord Mayor figure, the handle is formed as a bottle of 'Double Diamond' bass beer, around the front of base is printed 'Behind every great man'. The jug stands 8" high and was modelled by Mr Hallam in 1961, was withdrawn in 1970 and reintroduced in 1985. **Not particularly valuable**.

Willaim Ault (Tit Bits Toby)

Colour picture on page 99.

Made in 1917. It is a standing figure, 9¼" high. It was commissioned by George Newnes Ltd in 1917 for the Tit Bits magaine and were awarded as prizes in what was called 'Dittoes Competitions'. These jugs are made in an overall green enamel. Toby stands holding a grey open book on the cover of which is printed 'Tit Bits'. Around the base in raised letters is 'Tit Bits Toby Jug', these jugs were made by William Ault of Swandlincote, near Burton-on-Trent, Staffordshire. They are marked on the underside of the base:

'Ault-England'
(Reg applied for) or (662400)

Value approx £100/$180

The Peace Toby

Colour picture on page 99.

Is identical to the 'Tit Bits' Toby except that the cover of the book has been changed to read 'Peace 1919' and around the base, on the front in raised letters is '1914 Great War 1918'. The inside of the hat has been filled in, except for a ⅞" hole to accommodate a cork which is fixed to the jugs handle by a chain. The jug is painted in under glaze colours of chocolate brown, yellow browns and greens. Impressed mark 'Ault England 9'. Quite a rare Toby, only five recorded. **Value: £250/$450.**

Bass & Co also Homes Brewery

See under 'The Landlord'.

Buchanans Scotch Whiskey

A Toby in the form of a monk wearing a brown habit with a hinged lid. The inside of the jug is a pink colour and around the inside of the neck is printed 'Buchanans Scotch Whiskey'. Maker Falcome Pottery 1890-1905. **Value: under £100/$150**

Urn Toby

Colour picture on page 119.

A raised glass Toby was purchased in Spain at a car boot sale by Mrs Peets of Stockport in 1996. There is no inscription around the base, the jug is sealed at the top and on the bottom has been affixed a card with the message:

Within this jar repose the last remains
Catherine Hawkins 1929-1983
Author of "The Toby Jug"

Mrs Peets checked with her local library, who in turn checked with the British Museum and other sources in the UK and the USA, but no trace can be found of the lady's name or her book.

Maybe on reading this someone might shed some light on the mystery.

I've heard of Tobies being used for some unintended purposes, but never as a funeral urn, but to a dedicated Toby collector it's a wonderful idea. I'm thinking about it!

CHAPTER SIXTEEN

The Largest and the Smallest Tobies

The Largest

Colour picture on page 108.
It is thought that the largest Toby Jug to date is 39" high, made by Old Ellgreave Pottery of Burslem, in 1997. The photograph shows the original model from which the moulds were cast. The designer and decorator is Lionel Bailey's nineteen-year-old daughter Lorna and the modeller is Tony Cartlidge.

The jugs shows Toby holding a jug in his right hand and a pipe in his left. The figure has his mouth open laughing, showin his teeth and tongue. At the time of production it is thought that about six will be made, costing around £1000 each. Stephen Mullins of the Chicago, USA Toby Jug Museum was part responsible for this jug being made and for its sale and distribution.

Prior to the above jug, the largest known Toby Jugs to me were the ones some 24" high and marked Devonmoor. I have gained knowledge of nine of these jugs over the years, one in Poole, Dorset sitting damaged in a second hand shop some 20 years ago. Another, at the same time was sitting in a pub in Weymouth known as the smallest bar in Dorset. Paradoxically it housed the largest Toby Jug. In 1987 one was auctioned at J.M. Welch and Son in Great Dunmow, Essex. It sold for £500/$750 despite much repair to the hat. Another came up for auction in 1989, marked 'Devonmoor Pottery'. A large Toby of about the same height may be seen at the Toby Jug Restaurant at 40 High Street, Worthing in Sussex, made, for some reason, minus its handle by local pottery students c1974.

The jug with the most interesting history is owned by Stephan Mullins in Chicago, who has a jug museum and relates its history to date, he says:

"I bought it through a dealer who picked it up for me at a show in Detroit Michican. Copies of material found in the jug indicate a probable age of over 100 years.

How it got from the Schuch collection to a dealer in Detroit, I don't know. I paid $3300/£2200 (including dealers commission) plus $600/£400 for restoration (note comment about poor restoration)."

A letter found in jug:

This large Toby Jug shown in this photograph from my collection which is now in the senator John Schuch collection is to my knowledge and that of Marshall Fields of Chicago, the largest in the United States and possibly in the world, 23½" tall. It was in the potter's showroom in England for over fifty years, when it was imported by Marshall Field Inc. There it was used as a show piece for many years until purchased by me in 1940. It is without doubt over seventy-five years old. This photograph was taken in Kalamazoo June 1941.
> Signed C.L. Sherman.
> Director Mich. Hist. Museum.
> 18 December, 1948.

A further note in jug states:

A few years ago, someone attempted to steal this large Toby from the Schuch hotel. It was badly damaged in the attempt, the owner had it repaired by a local person that did a less than perfect job.

I feel some of the above dates are suspect. Although this jug is not marked I feel sure it was made by Devonmoor which did not start production until 1913.

See also the 'Falstaff Toby' by Staffordshire Fine Ceramics.

The Smallest

Colour picture on page 102.
The smallest ceramic Toby Jug believed to be made is ¹³⁄₁₆" high being currently manufactured in porcelain by Pauline and John Meredith of Badgers Mead, Hawthorn Hill, Bracknell, Berkshire, and is made for a doll's house. They also make

No longer the largest Toby at 23¼" high. Devonmoor c1913. £1000/$1750+.

three others: $^{15}\!/_{16}$", 1" and 1⅛" high. All three Tobies have blue coats, yellow breeches, white hose and black tricorn hats.

There are quite a number which are not as big as the normal size, ranging from around 1½" to around 7", as opposed to the normal size of 8" to 10". Without doubt, the Ralph Wood miniatures are the most desirable to acquire. These are 6" and 7" versions of their larger brothers either with the right hand on the small jug or alternatively holding a raised glass. The bases often tend to be proportionately higher than on larger jugs, and of course there are many potters of miniatures.

It may help the reader if we look at some of the variations, but it must of course be realised that these variations do not account for all the miniatures that can be found.

The standing miniature, clutching a foaming jug with both hands to his left breast, is probably Portobello ware c1830. Where the standing Toby holds a glass and bottle which is moulded to his body, one has to use one's own judgement as to the desirability of the piece, since they have been made in great numbers from the 1830s to the present day. The bases on these are quite high and the Tobies vary in height from 2" to 8".

The small Snuff Takers range from 4¾" to 5¼" in height. One of the small Snuff Taker types is 6¼", but he holds a large jug and a mug in place of the snuff-box.

There are other miniature Tobies 1½" high. Most of these are of the standing Toby, but there is also a 'Judy', a man with his hands in his pockets, and a woman with her hands on her hips. The woman may also be found with hands over her ears or on her lap, or the man holding a glass up in his right hand. One might be lucky

15 miniatures, the tallest is 5", c1830-50.

and find one of these little jugs with the Derby mark of the 'Stevenson & Hancock' period, made in 1861 at the earliest. These Tobies, around 1½" high, may be found marked 'Devonmoor'. They were made c1930.

None of the above tinies seem to have been made before this date. Quite a number are made in porcelain and bear a gold anchor mark whilst others may be found marked 'Crown Staffordshire'.

It has been said that all of these tinies were made as traveller's samples but there can be no truth in this as they bear little resemblance to a full size Toby. It follows the trend of calling many miniature antique items quite erroneously 'traveller samples'.

Other Toby Artefacts

Throughout the nineteenth century there were quite a number of household implements made with Toby in mind. Albeit, most were just as impracticable as the jug itself. These items are quite charming and, owing to the smallness of most of them, it contributes to their collectability.

See also colour pictures on pages 119, 120.

Condiments: Top row from left: egg cup; jam pot; and two ink wells. Bottom row from left: pen holder with three pepper pots.

Front, back and side views of flower wall holders. Twentieth century, said to have been made at Poole in Dorset.

CHAPTER EIGHTEEN

Inscriptions on Eighteenth and Nineteenth Century Toby Jugs

Ordinary Tobies	*Mirson* on base brown salt glaze jug; *O rare Dorset thou art my darling* on base.; *Tobey* on base.; *Charles Harding his Toby by God* on base; *1793 a fake date on front of base* late nineteenth century.; *Robt and Ann Wagstaff 1793* around base.; *Succefs to trade* on small jug on knee; *Not for you Boney* on small jug on knee.; *No No Bony not a drop* on small jug on knee; *Honest old Stingo* on small jug on knee; *Stingo* on small jug on knee; *William Manlay 1821* on front of base.; *B.T.* on small jug on knee; *William Coalbach His Jug / December 14 1833* impressed on bottom.; *Mild Ale* on small jug on knee; *Joseph Marttain, Bursslam* on front of base.; *Drink your ale up cock your tail up* on small jug on knee; *Peace* on small jug on knee; *Swansea Toby* late eighteenth century (Village Idiot); *Success to our wooden walls* on small jug on knee.; *George Baraclough 1835* on front of base; *Crispin Crispinas 1798* on small jug on knee (on ordinary) on small jug; *I.B.* raised initials on front of hat; *A Bumper / Milton / For Ever* on Yorkshire ordinary 1807 on small jug;
Long Faced Toby	*Ale* on small jug; *Monogram* at back.
Nelson	*Nelson* on front of base.
Shield Toby	*It is all out then fill him agian (sic)* on shield.
Hearty Good Fellow	*Hearty Good Fellow* on handle and front of base; *Stingo* on small jug; *Good Ale* on small jug; *Success to our wooden walls* on small jug; *Peace and Prosperity* on small jug; *with my jug in one hand and my pipe in the other* on front of base.
Sailor	*Lord Hou* under base.; *Dollars, jolly Jack Tar just come from far, drink round brave boys* Wood-type glazed Sailor; *Hallo, Brother Briton* on another wood-type Sailor; *Whoever thou may be / Sit down on that chest of / Hard dollars by me / And drink a health / To all sealors (sic) bold / Visct Jarvis / W.R.C. 'Old Toby' Grantham* inscribed on the base.
Sailor (Trafalgar)	*Trafalgar* at the back of a sea chest with a medallion of Nelson's Flagship *Victory*.
American Sailor (large and small)	*Success to our wooden walls* on small jug; *Dollers* on sea chest; *Victory medallion*
Lord Howe	*Lord Hou* on base; *Stingo on* left side of barrel, *Burton* on right side of barrel;
Rodney	*Make the fiddler drink for why / with fiddling he is dry* inscribed on coat; *J Marsh Jolley (Folley)* on base of two jugs.
John Bull	*Account* on paper held in hand.
Drunken Parson	*Strong ale* on small jug; *T. Burnell, London* under base.
Snuff Taker	*J.H. 1842 / Good health old chap* on Toby's waistcoat
Tithe Pig Parson Jug	*I will have no child tho the pig* on pillar; *Prince Hal* (silver lustre); *G.R.* on small shield; *John of Gant (sic)* on shield
Landlord Toby	*Home brewed ale* on front of barrel – A Toby sitting on a barrel on one end is inscribed Ale and on the other Stingo probably 'The Publican'.
Village Idiot	*John Barlow* on front of base.

CHAPTER NINETEEN

Eighteenth & Nineteenth Century Toby Jugs with Known Makers Marks

Maker's Names and Marks

Before c1840 impressed marks were neatly set into the soft clay during manufacture. The exception is salt-glaze stoneware such as Doulton's which was produced after this date with impressed marks.

It must be noted though that 95% of all early Tobies do not have any marks on them! Remember though, that although the mark is likely to be missing, the collector can develop his enthusiasm for Tobies by weighing up other indications as to the nature of the jug, by looking at the modelling, the 'feel', the glaze and other aspects aforementioned. However an early Toby bearing the maker's mark is a most desirable acquisition it not only proves both the maker and approximate date of the piece, but also allows us to use it as a guide to other unmarked jugs which have been made by the same potter. The presence of a mark thus adds value to the piece.

The most commonly marked pre-Victorian jugs are those marked 'Davenport'. These jugs were made at Longport, Burslem and the mark is usually impressed on the bottom of the jug with an anchor device beneath, though not all Davenport jugs are marked. On such jugs there are often two numerals showing the year of manufacture, situated on either side of the anchor.

The Davenport jugs are brightly coloured enamel Tobies, sometimes with gilding, and the bases are often stipple painted around the outside. This is also a feature of Portobelloware jugs and it is difficult to tell the difference between them since both potteries used the same kind of enamelling and colours and produced the jugs at around the same time c1830-40. Portobello jugs are unmarked.

On some early jugs it is not readily apparent whether a name on the underside of the jug is the potter or who the jug was made for. As a rule it would be the former and the recipients name would be on the front of the base, but there are probably exceptions.

C. Allerton	Matthew Knowles and Son	Sampson Smith
c1859-	c1835-1911	1851
Bourn & Son	Lakin and Poole	Spode
c1809-	c1791-1795	1783-1833
C.H. Branham	Leeds	Swansea
c1879-	c1775-1800	c1783-1833
S.A. & V. Briddon	Jacob Marsh (Foley)	Turner
c1848-1860	c1806-1834	c1770-
Copeland and Garret	Neale & Co	Walton
c1843-1847	1778-1814	c1818-1835
Copeland (Late Spode)	J. Oldfield & Co	Ralph Wood II
c1894-1910 (sail boat mark)	c1838-1888	1790-1795
Ruchard Darby	TH 1794	A rebus of three trees.
Sept 21 1787	Pearson & Co, Whittington Moore	R. Wood. V. Rare
Davenport	c1805-1879	c1770-90.
c1793-1887	A.C. Pope	Ralph Wood III
Derby (Stevenson and Hancock)	1829-	1795-1801
1861-	Reed & Taylor	Enoch Wood 'W'
Fulham John Carol	c1843-1850	Wood & Caldwell
c1885- (on brown saltglaze)	Rockingham	c1800
Hawley	c1826-1842	Pratt. Longport
1790-	Salt	1837 (this is a fake mark)
Thomas Hollins	c1820-1846	
1791-1820*	Thomas Sharpe	*Printed mirror-view on an Ordinary
William Kent	1821-1838	Toby
1878-1962 (old Staffordshire ware)		

CHAPTER TWENTY

Toby Jugs of British Personages

Classic Toby Jugs depict men generally, and women sometimes, in eighteenth century attire. Two hundred years later, it is not surprising that we see deviations from the standard form. Dress has been updated and the subject matter widened, so now it can be taken that any form, be it man or woman in any guise, may be termed a Toby jug so long as it includes a handle and an opening from which to pour.

Prices given in this book are limited to the very rare tobies, which is always of great interest. Otherwise there are just general references to value which are, (as are the prices of all antiques and collectables) open to market forces.

Name		Pottery	Date Designed	No made	
Lord Asquith	Prime Minister	Unknown	c1925		
Douglas Bader	Airman	Kevin Francis Ceramics	1990		Andrew Moss
Earl Baldwin	Prime Minister	Ashted	1990	1000	
Earl Baldwin	Prime Minister	unknown	c1925		
Hannah Barlow	Ceramic Artist	Kevin Francis Ceramics	1991		Geoff Blower
Earl Beatty	Sailor	Wilkinson Ltd	1917	350	Carruthers Gould
John Beswick	Potter	Kevin Francis Ceramics	1993		
Sgt Major Britain	Soldier	Melwood	1976	300	Allen Sly
Neville Chamberlain	Prime Minister	Wilkinson Ltd	c1939		Clarice Cliff
Neville Chamberlain	Prime Minister	Lancaster	1938		
Charlie Chaplin	Actor	Doulton	1918		
Winston Churchill	Prime Minister	W.H. Goss	1927		
Winston Churchill	Prime Minister	Doulton	1941 on.		H. Fenton (3 sizes)
Winston Churchill (seated)	Prime Minister	Burgess & Leigh	1941		E.T. Bailey
Winston Churchill (standing)	Prime Minister	Burgess & Leigh	1941		E.T. Bailey
Winston Churchill	Prime Minister	Copeland Spode	1945		Eric Olsen
Winston Churchill	Prime Minister	Kirkland (Etruria)	1941		
Winston Churchill	Prime Minister	Beswick	1941-45		Watkins
Winston Churchill	Prime Minister	W. Brannam	1941		
Winston Churchill	Prime Minister	Lancaster	c1941		Sandland
Winston Churchill	Prime Minister	Wilkinson Ltd	1941	400 approx	Clarice Cliff
Winston Churchill	Prime Minister	R.G. White	1941		
Winston Churchill	Prime Minister	Leonard Jarvis	1953		Leonard Jarvis
Winston Churchill	Prime Minister	Staffordshire Fine Ceramics	1987	1000	
Winston Churchill	Prime Minister	Kevin Francis Ceramics	1989		Peggy Davies
Small Churchill	Prime Minister	Kevin Francis Ceramics	1990		Peggy Davies
Winston Churchill (standing)	Prime Minister	Kevin Francis Ceramics	1989		Douglas V. Tootle
Winston Churchill (Never Despair)	Prime Minister				Douglas V. Tootle
Rev P.B. Tubby Clayton	Churchman	Ken C. Speaks	1959	6 only	
Clarice Cliff	Pottery Designer	Kevin Francis Ceramics	1990		Douglas V. Tootle
Susie Cooper					
Sir Stafford Cripps	Brit Ambassador	Burgess & Leigh	1941		E.T. Bailey
Peggy Davies		Kevin Francis Ceramics	1993		Douglas V. Tootle
Charles Dickens	Author	Burleigh Ware	c1950		
Sir Francis Drake	Sailor	Doulton	1981		M Abberley
Arnold Elliot	Publican	Melwood	c1974		
Lord French	Soldier	Wilkinson Ltd	1918	350	Carruthers Gould
Sir Lloyd George	Prime Minister	Wilkinson Ltd	1917	350	Carruthers Gould
Sir Lloyd George	Prime Minister	unknown	c1925		
W.E. Gladstone	Prime Minister	Sampson Smith	1870		
King George V		Wilkinson Ltd	1919	1000	Carruthers Gould
King Henry VIII		Staffordshire Fine Ceramics	c1985		Doc Paul Sing John Kay
King Henry VIII		Sylvac	c1955		
King Henry VIII		H. Wain and Sons	c1950		
King Henry VIII		Shorter and Son	c1950		
King Henry VIII		Kevin Francis Ceramics	1991		Geoff Blower
F.S. Hooker	Collector	Frank Stoner	c1912	6	Frank Stoner
Martha Gunn	Bathing attendant	Ralph Wood II	c1780		
Martha Gunn	Bathing attendant	Oldfield and Co	c1850		
Martha Gunn	Bathing attendant	Beswick (3½")	1948-66		
Martha Gunn	Bathing attendant	Wood and Sons	1973	1000	

Martha Gunn	Bathing attendant	Tony Wood (Studio 82) Ltd	c1980s		
Martha Gunn	Bathing attendant	Other unknown potters	c1780-1830		
Earl Haig	Soldier	Wilkinson Ltd	1917	350	Carruthers Gould
Lord Howe	Sailor	Ralph Wood II	c1780		
Lord Howe	Sailor	Wood and Sons	c1975	500	
Lord Howe	Sailor	Other unknown potters	c1780-c1820		
Lord Howe	Sailor	Beswick (3½")			
Earl Jellicoe	Sailor	Wilkinson Ltd	1916	350	Carruthers Gould
Dr S. Johnson	Writer	Enoch Wood	c1800		
Lord Kitchener	Soldier	Wilkinson Ltd	1915	250	Carruthers Gould
Sir Harry Lauder	Actor	unknown	c1925		
John Liston	Actor	Enoch Wood	c1825		
John Liston	Actor	Other potters	c1825		
Ramsey MacDonald	Prime Minister	unknown	c1925		
Lord Mackintosh	Industrialist and collector	Leonard Jarvis	1953	12 approx	Leonard Jarvis
John Major	Prime Minister	Kevin Francis Ceramics			
R.J. Mitchell	Designer of Spitfire aircraft	Wilkinsons Ltd	c1940	6 approx	Clarice Cliff
Lord Montgomery	Soldier	Manor	c1985		
Lord Montgomery	Soldier	Kevin Francis Ceramics	1990		Douglas V. Tootle
William Moorcroft	Potter	Kevin Francis Ceramics	1991		Douglas V. Tootle
Capt Henry Morgan	Pirate	Kevin Francis Ceramics			
Lord Nelson	Sailor	Various potters	19th C on.		
Sir John Peel	Huntsman	Wilkinsons Ltd	c1925		Clarice Cliff
Queen Elizabeth I		Staffordshire Fine Ceramics	c1985	1000	
Queen Elizabeth	The Queen Mother	Kevin Francis Ceramics	1990	900	Douglas V. Tootle
Charlotte Rhead	Ceramic Artist	Kevin Francis Ceramics	1991		Geoff Blower
George Robey	Actor	Doulton	1910-25		
Vic Schuler 8¾"	Collector	Kevin Francis Ceramics	1988	1000	Peggy Davies
Vic Schuler 6"	Collector	Kevin Francis Ceramics	1989	2500	Peggy Davies
Vic Schuler 9"	Collector	Kevin Francis Ceramics	1990	750	Douglas V. Tootle
Vic Schuler 4¼"	Collector	Kevin Francis Ceramics	1998		
Vic Schuler 4¾"	Collector	Kevin Francis Ceramics	1999		
Will Shakespeare	Playwright	Staffordshire Fine Ceramics	c1985		
Will Shakespeare	Playwright	Burleigh Ware	c1950		
Will Shakespeare	Playwright	Kevin Francis Ceramics	1990	1000	Geoff Blower
Margaret Thatcher	Prime Minister	Kevin Francis Ceramics	1989		Douglas V. Tootle
Lord Wavel	Soldier	Wilkinsons Ltd	c1940		
Josiah Wedgwood	Potter	Kevin Francis Ceramics			Douglas V. Tootle
Rev. George Whitfield	Churchman	Enoch Wood (others)	c1800 on.		
David Winter		Kevin Francis Ceramics			
Cardinal Wolsey	Churchman	H. Wain and Sons	1950s		
Ralph Wood	Potter	Kevin Francis Ceramics			

CHAPTER TWENTY-ONE

Toby Jugs of foreign personages made by British potters

General Botha	South African	Wilkinson Ltd	1918	250	Carruthers Gould
Stanley Bruce	Prime Minster Australia 1923-29	Ashstead Pottery	c1930		
Christopher Columbus	Artist	Kevin Francis Ceramics			Geoff Blower
Salvador Dali	Explorer	Kevin Francis Ceramics			
Cliff Cornell	US Industrialist	Doulton	1956		
General Eisenhower	US Soldier	Kevin Francis Ceramics			
Marshall Foch	Frenchman	Wilkinson Ltd	1918	350	Carruthers Gould
Mikhail Gorbachev	Russian Leader	Kevin Francis Ceramics	1990	1000	Andrew Moss
Oliver Hardy	US Film Star	Kevin Francis Ceramics			
Stonewall Jackson	US Civil War Soldier	Kevin Francis Ceramics			
Marshall Joffrey	French Soldier	Wilkinson Ltd	1918	350	Carruthers Gould
John F Kennedy	US President	Kevin Francis Ceramics			
Helmut Kohl	German Leader	Kevin Francis Ceramics	199?		
Sandra Kuck		Kevin Francis Ceramics			
Abraham Lincoln	US President	Staffordshire Fine Ceram	c1987	60	Dr Paul Sing
Nelson Mandela	S African Leader	Kevin Francis Ceramics			
Marx Brothers	US Film Stars	Kevin Francis Ceramics			
Napoleon	French Leader	Kevin Francis Ceramics			
General Patton	Soldier	Kevin Francis Ceramics			
Pavarotti	Italian opera singer	Kevin Francis Ceramics	1989	2000	Douglas V. Tootle
Picasso	Artist	Kevin Francis Ceramics			
Pope John Paul	Polish Churchman	Kevin Francis Ceramics	1990	1000	Douglas V. Tootle
Elvis Presley	US Singer	Kevin Francis Ceramics	1991	250	Andrew Moss
Field Marshall Rommel	German Soldier	Kevin Francis Ceramics	199?		
Field Marshall Rommel (standing figure)	Manor (pairs with General Montgomery)		c1985		
Franklin D. Roosevelt (very rare)	US President	Wilkinson Ltd	c1940s		
Franklin D. Roosevelt (*pairs with Winston Churchill*)	US President	Copeland Spode	1941		Eric Olsen
General Schwarzkopf	US Soldier	Kevin Francis Ceramics	1991	750	Andrew Moss
Stalin	Russian leader	Burgess and Leigh	1941		E. T. Bailey
(makes trio with Churchill and Stafford Cripps)					
Vincent van Gogh	Artist	Kevin Francis Ceramics			
Moe Widerman		Kevin Francis Ceramics			
Woodrow Wilson	US President	Wilkinson Ltd	1918	500	Carruthers Gould
Elihu Yale	Founder US Yale University	Wedgwood	1933		Prof Robert G. Eberherd
Boris Yeltsin	Russian Premier	Kevin Francis Ceramics			

CHAPTER TWENTY-TWO

Museums where Toby Jugs can be seen in Britain

London: Victoria and Albert Museum; British Museum; National Maritime Museum, Greenwich

Brighton, Sussex — Brighton Museum

Nottingham, Nottinghamshire — Nottingham Castle Museum

Cardiff, South Wales — National Museum of Wales

Edinburgh, Scotland — Royal Scottish Museum

York, Yorkshire — Yorkshire Museum

Hanley, Staffordshire — Stoke-on-Trent City Museum

Hull, Yorkshire — Hull City Museum (The Earle Collection)

Salisbury, Wiltshire — Salisbury Museum

Oxford, Oxfordshire — Ashmolean Museum

Liverpool, Merseyside — Merseyside County Museum

Portsmouth, Hampshire — Nelson Museum

CHAPTER TWENTY-THREE

Bibliography

Staffordshire Pottery Figures (1929) Herbert Read
British Toby Jugs Vic Schuler (1986 First Edition – 1994 Second Edition)
Astbury, Wheildon, Ralph Wood Figures and Toby Jugs (1922) Captain R.K. Price
Old English Toby Jugs (1949) Charles Platten Woodhouse FRSA
Toby Jugs (1968) John Bedford
Good Sir Toby (1955) Desmond Eyles
Character Jugs and Toby Jugs (1979) Desmond Eyles
The Mackintosh Collection of Fine Toby Jugs (May 1967) Sotheby & Co Auction Catalogue
English and Scottish Earthenware 1660-1860 (after 1958) G. Bernard Hughes
Staffordshire Chimney Ornaments (1955) Reginald Haggar
A Collector's Guide to Staffordshire Pottery Figures (1971) H.A.B. Turner
The Earle Collection of Early Staffordshire Pottery (1915) Cyril Earle
Jugs (1976) James Paton
The Wood Family of Burslem (1912) Frank Falkner
Collecting Antiques: Georgian Toby Jugs (1949) G. Bernard Hughes
Pratt Ware (1984) John & Griselda Lewis
Toby Jugs (Vol II of *Connoisseur Concise Encyclopedia of Antiques* 1959) Lord Mackintosh of Halifax
Staffordshire Pottery, The Tribal Art of England (1981) Anthony Oliver
The Antique Collectors Club Journal (May 1971)
Toby Jugs (in *Antiques Journal* — USA May 1947) Edward Wenham
Perhaps Bennington (*Antiques Journal* — USA April 1950) Gregor Norman Wilcox
Collecting Tobies (*The Antique Trader Weekly* — USA June 1978) William N McIntyre
Toby Fillpot and his Relations (Apollo c1955) Reginald G Haggar
An Impartial Look At Toby Jugs (in *Antique Dealers and Collectors Guide* Dec 1984) Anton Gabszewica
The Toby Jug — An Eighteenth Century Grotesque (*The Connoisseur* March 1904) D.C. Calthorp
Toby Jugs or Fillpots (*The Antique Dealer and Collector's Guide* April 1947) G.B. Hughes
Ralph Wood and His Contemporaries (Apollo April 1949) S.W. Fisher
Lure of the Toby Jug (*The Antique Dealer and Collector's Guide* Dec 1954) Arthur Grant
Toby Jugs (*Country Life* Dec 3 1959) G.B. Hughes
The Fun of Toby Jugs (*The Connoisseur* June 1954) Lord Mackintosh of Halifax
The Curious Tale of the Toby Jug G.B. Hughes
Toby Jugs are so English (*Art and Antiques* Oct 1971) Ronald Ellis and Barbara Pearce
A Toast to Toby Fillpot (*Art and Antiques* April 1975) C.G.L. DuCann
Toby Jugs — The Typical Englishman (*The Woman's Journal* 1984) Bevis Hiller
A Toast to Toby Jugs (*The Antique Trader* — USA Feb 27 1985) Morton B. Tobias
The British Toby (*Collector's World* Jan 1986) Francis Salmon
Toby Jugs — The Female of the Species (*Collector's World* Aug 1985) Vic Schuler
The Toby Jug (*The Royal Doulton International Collector's Club Magazine* Winter 1985) Kevin Pearson
The Wood Family Ceramics III (1986) Pat Halfpenny
Collecting Toby Jugs Sara Pozzo
The World of Antiques No 9 Summer 1991
The Toby & Character Jugs of the Twentieth Century and Their Makers (1999) David C. Fastenau and Stephen M. Mullins